Nymph-Fishing Rivers and Streams

Nymph-Fishing Rivers and Streams

A Biologist's View of Taking Trout Below the Surface

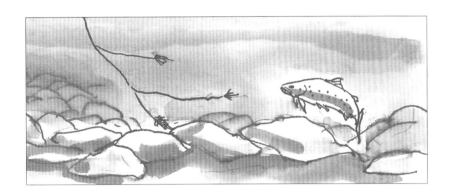

RICK HAFELE

STACKPOLE
BOOKS

Copyright © 2006 by Stackpole Books

Published by
STACKPOLE BOOKS
5067 Ritter Road
Mechanicsburg, PA 17055
www.stackpolebooks.com

Printed in China

First edition

10 9 8 7 6 5 4 3 2

Photographs by Rick Hafele, except where otherwise noted
Illustrations by Richard Bunse

Library of Congress Cataloging-in-Publication Data

Hafele, Rick.
    Nymph-fishing rivers and streams : a biologist's view of taking trout
below the surface / Rick Hafele.— 1st ed.
        p.   cm.
    Includes bibliographical references.
    ISBN-13: 978-0-8117-0169-3
    ISBN-10: 0-8117-0169-7
    1. Nymph fishing.   2. Rivers.   I. Title.

SH456.15.H34   2006
799.12'4—dc22
                                                                2005027278

To Dave Hughes,
whose encouragement made this book happen
and whose friendship has been
one of the few constants in my life.

CONTENTS

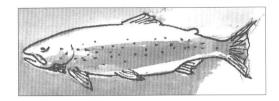

ACKNOWLEDGMENTS

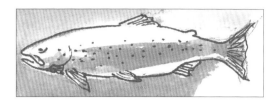

Although a single name appears on the cover, a book is never the product of a single person. Nothing could be truer in this case. In a very real sense, this book is the result of all those who have offered me knowledge and friendship over many years of fishing and studying streams. A number of fishing companions have played a special part, but I especially thank Dave Hughes, Richard Bunse, Jim Schollmeyer, Poul Bech, Dick VanDemark, John Smeraglio, and Skip Morris for sharing their great knowledge and wonderful friendship over many bumpy roads and rising trout.

Others have made major contributions to this effort. Special thanks go to John Smeraglio, owner of the Deschutes Canyon Fly Shop in Maupin, Oregon, for providing extensive help on fly patterns for nymphs, demonstrating several of the nymphing tactics pictured within, and making me laugh till my sides hurt. Thanks also to Richard Bunse for once again providing illustrations that show the true art and science of fly fishing and to Dave Hughes, Thomas Ames Jr., and Jeff Adams for their photos and helpful advice. And a big thank-you to Judith Schnell, Maria Metzler, and all those at Stackpole Books who gave this book life.

Finally, I thank my wife, Carol, who contributed time and effort editing and helping on the stream and has provided me major doses of love and understanding throughout this journey.

Thanks to all from the tips of my tarsi to the bottom of my heart.

INTRODUCTION

Authorities darken counsel. An authority is a person engaged in the invidious business of stereotyping and disseminating information, frequently incorrect . . . It was not until I realized this that my reading became any use to me. Up to that point I had been swallowing wholesale, with my facts, all sorts of fallacies and inaccuracies, alike in the matter of dressings and their use, and what they were intended to represent. From that point on an author became merely a suggester of experiment—a means of testing and checking my own observations by the water side, and no longer a small god to be believed in and trusted as infallible. And that is all an author, writing on any progressive art or science, ought to be.

GEORGE EDWARD MACKENZIE SKUES, *THE WAY OF A TROUT WITH A FLY*

Who needs another book on nymph fishing? This may be a strange question to ask at the beginning of a new book on the subject, but I feel compelled to ask it as I begin this project. If I am going to devote the time and energy required to write a book about nymph fishing, I want to do something that adds to the overall knowledge of the subject rather than just rehash what has already been said. Nymph fishing hasn't been the hottest topic in the fly-fishing world, but some excellent books have been written on the subject. A quick search for nymph-fishing books on the Internet turned up about fifteen titles on the subject. Some are among my favorite books on fly fishing, such as *Nymph Fishing for Larger Trout,* by Charles Brooks; *Tying and Fishing the Fuzzy Nymphs,* by E. H. "Polly" Rosborough; and *Nymphs,* by Ernie Schwiebert.

Clearly a lot of good information about nymph fishing has already been written. So where does this book fit in? Authors bring their own backgrounds and specialties to a subject. Mine are freshwater biology and the study of aquatic insects, which I've had the good fortune to be able to do professionally for nearly thirty years. My work has led me to look at aquatic insects, especially their nymphal stages, up close in all kinds of waters. It has also allowed me to look at how they behave, where they live, and how they become food for fish. The result has been a fascination with nymph fishing, a method I find very

effective and satisfying when I can successfully solve the underwater mystery that nymph fishing presents and downright fun when that mystery becomes a fish jumping out of the water on the end of my line.

So this is a book about nymph fishing from the perspective of an aquatic entomologist who has spent almost forty years trying to catch fish with flies. My goal is to explain what I've learned about nymphs and fish and how it translates to nymph-fishing methods that catch trout in streams and rivers anywhere in the world. The focus of this book is nymph fishing for trout—rainbow, brown, cutthroat, and brook. Most of the concepts and tactics, however, will be equally effective for other species of stream-dwelling sport fish, such as grayling, whitefish, and even smallmouth bass. No doubt some of the information presented here will be redundant with information already in print. But I hope that in the end, readers will gain new insights into the underwater world of nymphs and have a better idea of why and how to catch trout with their imitations.

What's a Nymph?

Like many words shared by science and fly fishing, the word *nymph* has two meanings: one technical, as used by entomologists, and another more general, as used by anglers. To entomologists, *nymph* refers to the immature

A key difference between nymphs and larvae is the presence or absence of wing pads. This mayfly nymph shows well-developed wing pads, common to insects that undergo incomplete metamorphosis.

This caddisfly larva, even when mature, will show no sign of wing pads. For insects that undergo complete metamorphosis, wing pads do not appear until the pupal stage.
DAVE HUGHES

stage of any insect with incomplete metamorphosis. That means those insects with three life stages: egg, nymph, and adult. Among aquatic insects, the orders Ephemeroptera (mayflies), Plecoptera (stoneflies), Odonata (dragonflies and damselflies), and Hemiptera (water boatmen and back swimmers) are the principal groups with incomplete metamorphosis. The immature stage of

insect orders with complete metamorphosis is technically called *larva*. These insects undergo four life stages: egg, larva, pupa, and adult. The main orders of aquatic insects with complete metamorphosis are Trichoptera (caddisflies), Megaloptera (alderflies and hellgrammites), Coleoptera (beetles), and Diptera (true flies, including mosquitoes, blackflies, and midges).

Most fly fishers use the word *nymph* to refer to the immature underwater stage of any aquatic insect. They also use the term to describe fly patterns that are fished underwater and imitate the nymphal or larval stages of aquatic insects. Because the word has multiple meanings, it is easy to get confused. Just remember that *nymph* and *larva* both refer to the immature stage of insects, and *nymph patterns* are designed to imitate them.

Insect Life Stages

Incomplete metamorphosis

- Egg
- Nymph
- Adult

Complete metamorphosis

- Egg
- Larva
- Pupa
- Adult

Aquatic insect orders with incomplete metamorphosis

- Mayflies
- Stoneflies
- Dragonflies and damselflies
- Water boatmen and back swimmers

Aquatic insect orders with complete metamorphosis

- Caddisflies
- Alderflies and hellgrammites
- Beetles
- Diptera

Why Fish Nymphs?

The answer to this question may seem obvious: We fish nymphs because they catch fish. But many other types of flies also catch fish, and many fly fishers who never use nymphs still catch plenty of fish. So why fish nymphs? Well, there are many times when fishing nymphs is the most effective way to catch fish, and in some situations it may be the only way you will catch fish. This is because fish spend considerable periods of time feeding exclusively on nymphal food forms underwater. Numerous studies have confirmed that 70 to 90 percent of a trout's diet is composed of insects in the underwater nymphal stages. So if you never use nymphs, you are missing out on numerous opportunities to increase your fishing success.

But there's another reason I fish nymphs. I find it a grand mystery. Think about it: When fishing dry flies, you see where and how the fish are feeding and what they are feeding on, and thus you know what fly you should use. You also see how the insects are behaving and thus know how you should present your fly. Everything—well, most everything—is quite obvious. The challenge then becomes executing your technique: picking the correct pattern and presenting it so fish believe it's the real thing. With nymph fishing, the where, what, and how are underwater and can't be seen. They're a mystery that requires deciphering if you are going to be successful. And to decipher this mystery consistently, you need to understand what's happening underwater—where fish feed, when they feed, how they feed, and what's available for them to eat. Then you need to apply the correct techniques to get an effective pattern in front of feeding fish in a natural-looking way. And finally, you need to be able to tell when a fish has taken your fly. To me, this is why nymph fishing is so interesting and challenging.

Nymph fishing is like a puzzle, and the pieces to this puzzle are there for those who are willing to look and know what they are seeing.

It is the intention of this book to help you put together the pieces of this puzzle so you will be able to successfully fish nymphs wherever and whenever they are needed. But as G. E. M. Skues said, don't automatically believe everything you read in this or any other book. Try the methods, experiment with different ones, and compare the ideas with your own experiences. Discover for yourself what works and what doesn't. Such self-discovery is the real home of knowledge. Finally, I hope you gain new appreciation for nature in general, and in particular for the incredible mysteries of life unfolding under the surfaces of all rivers and streams.

Happy casts and happy nymphing!

CHAPTER ONE

In the Beginning

Around the steel no tortur'd worm shall twine,

No blood of living insect stain my line;

Let me, less cruel, cast feather'd hook,

With pliant rod athwart the pebbled brook,

Silent along the mazy margin stray,

And with fur-wrought fly delude the prey.

JOHN GAY

Nymph fishing spans the entire history of fly fishing, although there is considerable debate over just when fly fishing itself began. The first references to fishing with hooks that had some sort of feathers attached go back thousands of years. Some of the earliest records are from China, about three thousand years ago during the Shang dynasty. The first written description of a fishing reel is also from China, about eleven hundred years ago during the Sung dynasty. But it was Claudius Aelianus, a Roman stationed in Macedonia (part of today's Northern and Central Greece) in the late second and early third century A.D., who gave the first description of fly fishing on streams. No one knows whether these first fly fishers had much knowledge of the underwater stages of insects and were consciously imitating nymphs, but given the nature of materials available at the time, it is probable that they were fishing flies that sank underwater—in other words, wet flies or nymphs. Another thousand years passed before fly fishers figured out how to get flies to float when needed. Thus one could say that all fly fishers were nymph fishers for the first thousand years of the sport, even if it was by default.

The first book specifically about fly fishing is generally considered to be *The Treatys of Fysshynge wyth an Angle,* written by the prioress of an English nunnery named Dame Juliana Berners and published in 1496. Though it did not describe nymph fishing specifically, this book, now more than five hundred years old, gives good descriptions of both wet and dry flies. Her book also started a long line of fly-fishing literature from England and the British Isles. Still, information linking the underwater stages of insects to fly patterns was scant at best until 1600, when John Taverner wrote *Certaine Experiments Concerning Fish and Fruite.* Taverner made it clear that the underwater aquatic stages of insects were an important food for trout and that flies could be used to imitate them. But the real breakthrough came in 1836, when Alfred Ronalds, another Englishman, published *The Fly-Fisher's Entomology.* Ronalds was a biologist and is considered the first to have systematically studied the habits of aquatic insects and connected those habits to the flies and techniques for fly fishing. This is a seminal work and still worth a read today if you have the good fortune of finding a copy.

To me, however, the most important writer on the subject of nymphs and nymph fishing, past or present, came about seventy-five years later. I'm speaking of George Edward MacKenzie Skues, who fished the famed chalkstreams of southern England, primarily the Itchen, at a time when dry flies were considered the only "true"

G. E. M. Skues developed his understanding of nymphs and nymph fishing on English chalkstreams. These fertile waters were perfect places to observe insects and fish and test new ideas. DARREL MARTIN

method of fly fishing. Frederic Halford was the main proponent of the dry-fly-only mentality, and his views spread widely with the publication of his books *Floating Flies and How to Dress Them* (1886) and *The Dry-Fly Man's Handbook* (1913). Halford honed his views on the River Test, perhaps the most famous of the English chalkstreams. In the late 1800s and early 1900s, however, Skues was fishing the Itchen, just a short cast from Halford and the Test, and fortunately didn't blindly buy into the dry-fly-only idea.

Skues was a great observer, and he observed on many occasions fish feeding underwater, often selectively. This even happened when adult insects were on the surface during a hatch. As a result, Skues studied the underwater nymphs and developed flies and techniques to imitate them. He also happened to be an excellent writer and explained his observations quite eloquently in several books, two of which are every bit as important and interesting to read today as when they were written. These are *Minor Tactics of the Chalk Stream* (1910) and *The Way of a Trout with a Fly* (1921). Copies of these books can still be found, and I highly recommend them.

Halford died in 1914, but in his later years, he had quite heated—and now famous—debates with Skues over

the use of wet flies and nymphs. These debates almost had a religious fervor, with Halford arguing that fly fishing was fly fishing only when done with a floating fly. Both were persuasive men, and it is hard to say that either won the argument. In fact, in some ways this debate continues to this day. Many a modern fly fisher will contest that nymph fishing isn't really fly fishing, that it somehow takes on the nature of bait fishing or is a cruder form of the fine art of fishing with a fly. Such feelings run deep and can be traced back to the debates of the late nineteenth century between Halford and Skues.

If you feel at all negative about the ethics of nymph fishing, I strongly encourage you to read one of Skues's books. A little poem from *The Way of a Trout with a Fly* illustrates both his point of view and his sense of humor:

Oh, thrilling the rise to the lure that is dry
When the shy fish comes up to his slaughter
Yet rather would I have
The turn to my fly,
With a cunning brown wink under water.
The bright little wink under water!
Mysterious wink under water!

Delightful to ply
The subaqueous fly,
And watch for the wink under water!

Skues's books greatly influenced other English and American angling writers who followed him. Three that need mention in the evolution of nymph fishing are J. R. Harris, who wrote *An Angler's Entomology* (1952); Frank Sawyer, with his book *Nymphs and the Trout* (1958); and Major Oliver Kite, who wrote *Nymph Fishing in Practice* (1963). Harris's book, built on the work of Ronalds, added considerable information to the understanding of aquatic insects in the British Isles. He not only described in detail most mayfly, stonefly, and caddisfly hatches, but also addressed lesser insects such as dragonflies and damselflies, true flies (Diptera), and even crustaceans. The book provides a wealth of detailed information about insect behavior, distribution, and fly patterns, and though it addresses only insects of Great Britain, it provides a template for understanding and describing insect hatches anywhere. Frank Sawyer, a famous river keeper on the River Avon, took Skues's ideas and further refined the flies and techniques. Sawyer made a strong argument that nymph fishing required more skill and knowledge than dry-fly fishing. Major Oliver Kite acknowledged the importance of Skues and Sawyer and provided insightful information about the life cycles, habits, and behavior of numerous nymphs of southern England streams.

These writers and others from Great Britain added a tremendous amount of information to the world of fly fishing. Many ideas that we take for granted can be traced back to these early pioneers of the sport. But beginning in the early 1900s, North America experienced its own advancement in fly-fishing knowledge and literature, and given the influence of English writers of the time, many ideas paralleled what was happening in England. Some American anglers advocated dry flies as the only appropriate method of fly fishing; others looked deeper to the life below the surface and created successful nymphs and methods of fishing them that fit the unique conditions of the streams and fish species in America.

Early American fly-fishing writers honed their techniques in the streams of the Pocono and Catskill Mountains. The primary trout species in these streams at the time was native brook trout. Most of these streams presented considerably different conditions than the clear, slow-flowing chalkstreams of southern England, which were inhabited by brown trout. As a result, early American fly fishers had to adapt the methods described by English writers to their own setting.

Perhaps the first significant fly-fishing writer in America was Thaddeus Norris. He primarily fished the Brod-

heads in the Pocono Mountains and wrote *The American Angler's Book* (1864). Besides being one of the earliest noted fly fishers of American waters, Norris was also one of the first great bamboo rod makers of the nineteenth century. Most bamboo rods in England were made with a three-strip construction at the time, but Samuel Phillippe, a close friend of Norris's, developed the first modern six-strip design, and Norris became expert in its construction. Such rod designs made fly fishing much more effective and pleasurable. It also made the large native brook trout of eastern streams more vulnerable to fishing pressure.

The twenty years following the Civil War were perhaps the pinnacle of fly fishing for large native brook trout in their native streams. By the late 1800s, uncontrolled clear-cutting for lumber and clearing the land for orchards and farms radically altered the water quality and spelled the end of some great fishing. Two hundred years later, history appears to be repeating itself in the great salmon rivers of the Pacific Northwest, where logging, agriculture, dams, and urban sprawl produce water quality and habitat changes that threaten what once were the greatest runs of salmon in the world.

Other writers sprang from the fertile waters of the northeastern mountains in the late 1800s, but it was Theodore Gordon, a fly tier, not a writer, who is perhaps best remembered. His best-known fly, the Quill Gordon, shows the art of form and function that became the standard goal for dry flies in America. It seems that the early writers and tiers in America focused on fishing dry flies as exemplified by Emlyn Gill's *Practical Dry-Fly Fishing* (1912), and George LaBranche's *Dry Fly in Fast Water* (1914). LaBranche also discussed flies and techniques for fishing below the surface, but it was Edward Ringwood Hewitt who wrote one of the first books on nymph fishing in America, titled *Nymph Fly Fishing* (1934). Hewitt applied many of Skues's ideas to the specific insects he found in his favorite river, the Neversink. Close on the heels of Hewitt's little book came Ray Bergman's *Trout* (1938). This seminal work covered all fly-fishing techniques, including nymph fishing, and became a must-read for American fly fishers.

More serious books on nymph-fishing American waters began to emerge in the 1940s and 1950s. One of the first was written by James Leisenring, a Pennsylvania angler noted more for his fishing skill than his writing ability. With the help of fellow angler Vernon S. "Pete" Hidy, he produced an important but not well-known book, *The Art of Tying the Wet Fly* (1941). Though Leisenring died in 1951, twenty years later, in 1971, Hidy reintroduced the book under the title *The Art of Tying the Wet Fly and Fishing the Flymph,* with both Leisenring and Hidy listed as authors. Leisenring was a keen observer and corresponded regularly with Skues in England. As a result, he used the ideas of Skues and other English writers such as Stewart to develop methods for tying and fishing sunken flies in his home waters. The Leisenring lift is to this day a commonly described method of fishing nymphs and wet flies, and his patterns also persist in the many wet flies and soft-hackles still in common use. In the same year that Leisenring died, another key nymph-fishing book was published by Ray Ovington, titled *How to Catch Trout on Wet Flies and Nymphs*. Ovington was a close friend of Edward Sens, an important fly tier and angler in the Catskills. Sens developed a set of nymph patterns designed to complement each of the best-known dry-fly patterns of the area. He also developed effective nymph-fishing techniques. Sens was not a writer, however, and his methods weren't described in print until Ovington compiled them in his book on the subject.

Eastern writers, writing about eastern hatches and streams, provided the focal point for all the fly-fishing books mentioned above. Western streams, however, had some of the best trout fishing in the country, if not the world, and the types of insects and streams were quite different from those found in the East. Thus, though east-ern fly patterns and methods could be successful, western anglers developed their own patterns and methods for western streams. One of the first books on nymph patterns and techniques specifically for western waters was E. H. "Polly" Rosborough's *Tying and Fishing the Fuzzy Nymphs* (1969). Like the important anglers before him, Polly's patterns and methods stemmed from direct observation and experience on his home waters. Polly began fishing in northern California but later moved to southern Oregon, where he fished streams filled with insects and fat rainbows, including the Williamson and Wood Rivers. His book is a great example of how careful observation of the natural insects shapes effective fly patterns. This was followed in 1976 by another important book on nymph fishing for western waters: *Nymph Fishing for Larger Trout*, by Charles E. Brooks. Charlie Brooks lived in West Yellowstone and fished the great trout waters of Montana, Wyoming, and Idaho. These big, dashing rivers and the large, dancing trout they harbored influenced his flies and methods. And as with the English and eastern writers before him, Charlie's observation of natural insects and their habits was the key to his success and is why his book is still important today.

Large western rivers required different flies and methods than the smaller, gentler streams of England and the eastern streams of America.

In between these two works, a rather amazing book on nymph fishing was published by another eastern writer and angler. Ernest Schwiebert's *Nymphs* (1973) is remarkable for both the scope and detail in which he covers this subject for the angler. Thirty-six chapters describe the nymphal stages of all the major aquatic insect orders and freshwater crustaceans at the level of individual species, including information on their behavior, patterns and fishing methods, and hundreds of black-and-white and color drawings. It is truly a daunting undertaking that some anglers may find overly filled with Latin names, but there is no doubt in my mind that this book took the concept of nymph fishing to new dimensions. Early in this book, Schwiebert makes eloquent arguments for the importance of fishing nymphs:

> Using just any nymph pattern when fish are taking nymphal forms cannot work. The flies must be accurate imitations of the naturals. It is surprising to find that men who fully understand selectivity in its context of dry-fly imitations and adult insects are often unaware of selectivity to wet flies and nymphs. Trout can examine subsurface foods readily, without the distortions of the surface film and broken current patterns, and see them better than diet-forms on the surface; and therefore trout are perhaps more selective to nymphs in terms of color, configuration, and size than they are to dry flies fished in the mirrorlike meniscus.

Schwiebert then provides more than three hundred pages of information about hundreds of nymphs—where they live, how they behave, patterns to imitate them, and how to fish the patterns. Since *Nymphs* was published, much more has been discovered about aquatic insects, and many of their Latin names have been changed as entomologists describe new species and revise the taxonomy, but this book still remains a decisive work about nymphs and nymph fishing.

The intervening years since *Nymphs* was published have seen other books devoted to nymph fishing. Major fly-fishing writers including Dave Whitlock, Gary Borger, and Dave Hughes have written about nymphs and nymph fishing, and books such as Doug Swisher and Carl Richards's *Selective Trout* (1971), Al Caucci and Bob Nastasi's *Hatches* (1975), and Gary LaFontaine's *Caddisflies* (1981) have added greatly to our knowledge of nymphs and patterns to match them. But to me, Schwiebert's *Nymphs* provides a logical stepping-off point between the history of nymph fishing and more current ideas on tackle, patterns, and techniques. The history of nymph fishing is rich with innovative thinkers and writers. Nevertheless, some anglers today still have narrow views about what constitutes "real" fly fishing and question the use of nymphs. I worry little about anglers with such views. I just think back to G. E. M. Skues and remember how simply he put it:

> Delightful to ply
> The subaqueous fly,
> And watch for the wink under water!

Nymph Fishing Today

Nymph fishing in the twenty-first century has evolved into a fine art. Based on the number of magazine articles about nymph fishing and the number of people I see on streams fishing nymphs, it seems clear that nymph fishing is now a mainstream part of the sport. A major reason is the success that experienced anglers have fishing nymphs. Even anglers who don't fish nymphs or get frustrated fishing them generally agree that nymph fishing is important. If you need more proof, just look at the number of guides who rig their clients for nymph fishing versus dry-fly fishing. Sure, during a hatch, dry flies are fun and effective, but guides need their clients to catch fish the other 80 percent of the time as well.

Another reason is that our understanding of fish and the food on which they feed has never been better. During the past thirty or forty years, fish biologists and aquatic entomologists have gained a tremendous amount of knowledge about basic behavior, life cycles, and habitat preferences of fish and insects. Thus anglers have better information on which to base pattern design and selection and the tactics for presenting their flies.

Finally, there has never in the history of the sport been such a large range of equipment available to fish more effectively. Rods and lines are available for every conceivable water type and tactic. Anglers also have a multitude of choices in leaders, strike indicators, and weight designed to maximize success. This is a double-edged sword, as all the refinement and the multitude of choices can lead to confusion as much as success. This book will help make sense of a lot of these choices now available, but experience and practice are the final teachers in any learning process.

A brief summary of the milestones and key players in the history of fly fishing generally and nymph fishing in particular:

- 2000 B.C. References to fishing with hooks covered with feathers found in ancient Chinese documents.

- 200 A.D. The Roman, Claudius Aelianus, provides the first description of fly fishing in streams of Macedonia.

- 1496. Dame Juliana Berners, *The Treatys of Fysshynge wyth an Angle.*

- 1600. John Taverner, *Certaine Experiments Concerning Fish and Fruite.*

- 1651. Thomas Barker, *The Art of Angling.*

- 1653. Sir Izaak Walton, *The Compleat Angler.*

- 1676. Charles Cotton, *Being Instructions How to Angle for a Trout or Grayling in a Clear Stream.*

- 1747. Richard Bowlker, *The Art of Angling.*

- 1836. Alfred Ronalds, *The Fly-Fisher's Entomology.*

- 1857. William Stewart, *The Practical Angler.*

- 1864. Thaddeus Norris, *The American Angler's Book.*

- 1886. Frederic Halford, *Floating Flies and How to Dress Them.*

- 1910. George Edward MacKenzie Skues, *Minor Tactics of the Chalk Stream.*

- 1912. Emlyn Gill, *Practical Dry-Fly Fishing.*

- 1913. Frederic Halford, *The Dry-Fly Man's Handbook.*

- 1914. George LaBranche, *Dry Fly in Fast Water.*

- 1919. Francis Ward, *Animal Life Underwater.*

- 1921. George Edward MacKenzie Skues, *The Way of a Trout with a Fly.*

- 1934. Edward Ringwood Hewitt, *Nymph Fly Fishing.*

- 1938. Ray Bergman, *Trout.*

- 1939. George Edward MacKenzie Skues, *Nymph Fishing for Chalkstream Trout.*

- 1941. James Leisenring, *The Art of Tying the Wet Fly.*

- 1951. Ray Ovington, *How to Catch Trout on Wet Flies and Nymphs.*

- 1952. J. R. Harris, *An Angler's Entomology.*

- 1958. Frank Sawyer, *Nymphs and the Trout.*

- 1960. Jim Quick, *Fishing the Nymph.*

- 1963. Major Olive Kite, *Nymph Fishing in Practice.*

- 1969. E. H. "Polly" Rosborough, *Tying and Fishing the Fuzzy Nymphs.*

- 1971. Doug Swisher and Carl Richards, *Selective Trout.*

- 1973. Ernie Schwiebert, *Nymphs.*

- 1975. Al Caucci and Bob Nastasi, *Hatches.*

- 1976. Charles Brooks, *Nymph Fishing for Larger Trout.*

- 1979. Gary Borger, *Nymphing: A Basic Guide to Identifying, Tying, and Fishing Artificial Nymphs.*

- 1981. Rick Hafele and Dave Hughes, *The Complete Book of Western Hatches.*

- 1981. Gary LaFontaine, *Caddisflies.*

- 1982. Dave Whitlock, *Guide to Aquatic Trout Foods.*

- 1995. Dave Hughes, *Nymph Fishing.*

CHAPTER TWO

The Trout

*Now, if I want to catch a trout, first I must know where there are some
to catch, or neither you nor myself can catch any. If I want to catch a
big trout I must first locate a big one or be content with smaller ones.*

JAMES LEISENRING AND PETE HIDY,
THE ART OF TYING THE WET FLY AND FISHING THE FLYMPH

Trout are moving targets. They may be feeding on nymphs in shallow riffles in the morning and sipping spinners in quiet eddies in the afternoon. Feeding periods and locations vary with changing water conditions, weather, and insect activity, so you can't assume that what you see fish doing today will be what they are doing tomorrow. As a result, it is difficult to come up with a simple formula that will consistently tell you where fish will be feeding.

Habitat and What Trout Need

To be a successful nymph fisher, you need to understand basic trout behavior, habitat preferences, and how these change under different conditions. A good place to start is with an understanding of what trout need to survive.

To best understand trout behavior, try observing it directly from underwater. A mask, snorkel, and wet suit can open up the underwater world like nothing else. Once you enter the water, fish seem to have little fear of you, and you can watch their natural behavior from close range. I have actually touched trout from underwater before they swam away.

Protection from Predators

Finding food and avoiding becoming food are two critical factors in the survival of any wild creature, and avoiding predators is usually more important than finding food. Most animals can go a few days without food, but one little slipup in the "being eaten" category and the game is over. Thus finding cover and protection from predators is the number-one skill for fish to learn. This is especially true for young juvenile fish. At this stage, they are smaller and slower than many other creatures both under the water and above, which makes them ideal food for a long list of bigger animals, including larger fish, frogs, snakes, kingfishers, herons, and on and on. Little trout learn quickly to hide in thick cover or they soon become a different part of the food chain.

The risk of moving up the food chain exists even for mature trout. During a float down the Bighorn River in Montana, I saw a great blue heron dragging a brown trout of at least sixteen inches out of the water. The trout was much too big for the heron to fly away with, but it had no intention of catch-and-release. In the end, any trout that reaches a size of interest to an angler has mastered the art of detecting and hiding from potential predators. It is a bit like a game of hide-and-seek but with a much higher penalty for losing.

Protection from the Current

Part of the beauty of trout is their perfect design for life in moving water. Without any apparent effort, they hang in the current or dart to one side or another to grab a morsel of food. If you are snorkeling, you can observe this firsthand. Where you have to grab on to rocks and struggle to

With a wet suit, mask, and snorkel, you can observe the underwater world of the trout firsthand.

Trout seen from underwater while snorkeling show little alarm and allow you to come quite close.

River otters are great fun to watch—unless you're a trout.

Trout use more energy to stay put in heavy fast water, but such water also provides more food.

stay put in the current, trout sit almost motionless. Slight twitches of a pectoral or ventral fin seem to be the only signs that they are working to adjust to the many fingers of current below the surface. But remaining stationary in any current requires effort, which equates to energy expended. Many streams and rivers have major sections dominated by swiftly moving water, such as the Madison River in Montana. In such habitats, trout have to expend even more energy to deal with the fast current. Therefore, they need to find areas where the current is broken and slowed. These areas provide critical resting spots, reducing the trout's energy requirements and thus the amount of food necessary to survive. Just as a long-distance runner needs more calories to maintain his or her weight than does a writer sitting behind a computer all day, a trout in fast water has greater caloric requirements than one resting out of the current. The advantage of fast water is that it carries more food, so trout are constantly balancing the need to swim out into the current to feed with the need to get out of the current to conserve energy.

Food

Eventually every animal must leave the safety of its home to find food. Most people leave home and move into the dangerous current of a freeway in order to work and earn money to buy food. Trout also leave the safety of home, like a nice deep pool or safe spot under an old log, and move out into the stream's current where the grocery shelves are better stocked. The prime feeding areas are the places with the highest concentrations of food. When trout are feeding on the surface, it is possible to see where the food is most abundant and where the fish are feeding. When you're fishing nymphs, however, you can't see the food or the trout and therefore must picture in your mind where food might be most prevalent. This is one of the keys to improving your nymph-fishing success.

To understand where food is concentrated underwater, it helps to look where it is concentrated on the surface. As surface food floats downstream, small surface currents push it in certain directions, often concentrating it into narrow lanes. We call these feeding lanes

because of the way trout position themselves underneath them. Feeding lanes are most pronounced where surface currents form distinct lanes of different current speeds. Water deflected around boulders or logs and areas near banks, especially on the outside bends of meanders, typically produce well-defined current or feeding lanes. Eddies, where the current rotates in a slow, circular pattern, also concentrate food. Well-defined current lanes form along the outside edges of eddies, but even more important is how surface food gets trapped within the body of the eddy by the swirling currents. The end result is that eddies provide slow current and concentrated food, two reasons why large trout like eddies so much.

The same types of current or feeding lanes that form on the surface also form underwater, and they form around the same types of structure. Currents deflected around boulders or logs, along the edges of banks, and in or around eddies all create underwater feeding lanes. In fact, wherever you see current lanes on the surface, there will usually be similar current lanes underwater in the same area. The big difference is that underwater currents are three-dimensional instead of two-dimensional like surface currents. Boulders and logs that are submerged several feet below the surface may not create a current lane on the surface, but they will create one along the stream bottom. Food is concentrated in these underwater feeding lanes just as it is on the surface. Trout feeding on nymphs know the locations of these underwater feeding lanes, and the biggest trout take the best ones.

Whenever you fish nymphs or subsurface flies, look closely at the stream bottom for features or underwater obstructions that create feeding lanes. Try to estimate how far below the surface these feeding lanes occur, and then get your flies to drift right down the lanes like you would with a dry fly on the surface. You can even play a game I call "I know you're in there." Here's how it goes.

When I start nymph-fishing a section of stream, I pick out the areas I feel will produce the best underwater feeding lanes and try to visualize exactly where trout will be holding in these lanes. Then I make a presentation so that my fly drifts down the feeding lane at the right depth to

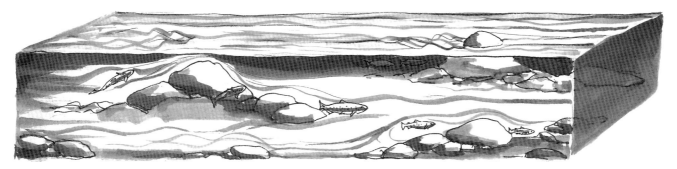

Boulders and bottom contours create underwater feeding lanes that concentrate food for trout feeding below the surface.

Trout often congregate around logs and wood debris.

pass in front of my imagined feeding trout. I pretend each cast is to a feeding trout in an underwater lane, just as if I were casting to a trout feeding on the surface. To play the game, I keep track of how often I get a strike at the spot where I expected a trout to be feeding. I win when I get a strike, and the trout win when I don't. Though the trout win most of the time, I win a lot more often than if I were casting randomly into the water. I also learn more about where trout are and where they're not, because I am picking out very specific places to fish. When I'm right, I can quickly locate another spot with similar current and depth characteristics and have a much higher probability of being right again, thereby improving my skill at locating fish in the process.

Logs slow the current and provide cover for trout and other fish.

Key Habitat Features

Where all three of the main ingredients trout seek—protection from predators, protection from the current, and food—occur together, you have, in angler speak, a hot spot. Hot spots change as conditions change from day to day or season to season or even with time of day, but habitat that provides the three main ingredients will consistently hold trout. If you learn to recognize key habitat features that meet the prime needs of trout, you will remove a lot of the guesswork involved in reading the water and find hot spots more frequently. There are several habitat features that provide important ingredients and consistently attract trout.

Logs and Wood Debris. Logs and wood debris produce some of the best habitat for all types of fish. Remember those stories about the giant trout under an old fallen log? Some were actually true. It isn't surprising that logs and wood debris attract fish. First, they make it nearly impossible for terrestrial predators, such as herons, kingfishers, and anglers, to see the fish from above the water, so they offer great protection. For the angler, even when you can see that big trout under the log, it is often next to impossible to get your fly close without getting snagged on a log or branch. If you do manage to drift your fly near the trout and it actually takes your fly, the trout has so many nearby branches or snags to swim around that landing it is next to impossible. Second, logs deflect the current, giving trout a place to rest out of its main force. Third, by deflecting the current, logs and wood debris create numerous eddies, pools, or backwaters that can attract or concentrate food. Thus logs and wood debris provide all three key ingredients for trout. Streams may or may not have a lot of logs and wood in them, but wherever you see wood in a stream, stop and give it a careful look for that big trout lurking nearby.

Undercut Banks. Undercut banks provide some of the same benefits as logs and wood debris. A trout tucked back under a bank is well hidden from view and therefore safe from many predators. Undercut banks also slow the current and, depending on how the current is moving, may concentrate food. Deep undercut banks on the outside bend of a stream meander generally provide better habitat than shallow undercuts with little current. When fishing along undercut banks, it is not always necessary to drift your fly back into the undercut to catch fish. Drifting your fly along the edge will often entice a hard strike.

Other Banks. Many types of banks provide good habitat. The current slows near banks because of the friction along the shore, and more food is present because of the added insects falling in from shoreline vegetation. Protection from predators may be lacking unless cover from overhanging shrubs or trees is present. One of the most common mistakes anglers make is wading into the water without first looking carefully along the bank for trout. If you step into the water, you will spook any trout nearby. I

Large trout often like the security and safety of undercut banks.

Banks concentrate food from below and above. Always look closely for feeding trout along banks with some depth and cover.

have caught some very nice trout by standing out of the water and drifting a nymph near shore with only a few feet of fly line on the water. The best banks are those where the depth increases quickly to two or three feet and there is cover in or above the water where trout can hide or escape the current.

Boulders. Boulders are one of the most common habitat features in streams and rivers. In general, they are defined as rocky substrate over ten inches in diameter. I think of them as any rock larger than a bowling ball. The size and number of boulders in a stream depend on the type of rock along the stream channel, the stream's gradient or slope, and the amount and velocity of water. More boulders occur in steep channels with fast water, which washes smaller rocks downstream. To trout, boulders provide key places to get out of the current in fast-water sections of streams. Not only does the current slow directly below a boulder, but there also is a cushion of slow water directly in front of it. As trout like to feed near fast-water areas, boulders provide them important relief from the current. Surface turbulence around boulders also provides some cover or protection from predators.

Slack water behind and in front of boulders provides trout with great places to rest and gather food.

Fishing nymphs around patches of boulders is almost always a good idea.

Yes, trout really do sit in front of boulders.

In moderate to fast-water sections of streams, boulders create what is commonly called pocket water. This water can hold a lot of trout that rarely get fished over. Though trout will rise to surface flies in pocket water, it usually takes a good hatch to produce consistent activity on the surface. Most trout focus on nymphs and larvae drifting in the fast current. Dropping a nymph pattern in and around the pockets can be very effective.

Eddies. Eddies form where the shape of the bank, boulders, logs, or other structure deflects the current into a slow, circular pattern. Their size can vary from one to over fifty feet across. Eddies concentrate and trap food in their swirling currents and have slow water, two factors that always attract trout. The turbulence caused by conflicting currents around the edges of eddies often produces foam. Pay particular attention to such areas as many insects, both adults and emerging nymphs, get caught in the foam. Trout will hang in the water just below the foam and feed leisurely on all the easy-to-catch food. Besides trapping food, the foam provides overhead cover from predators. Because large eddies do not always

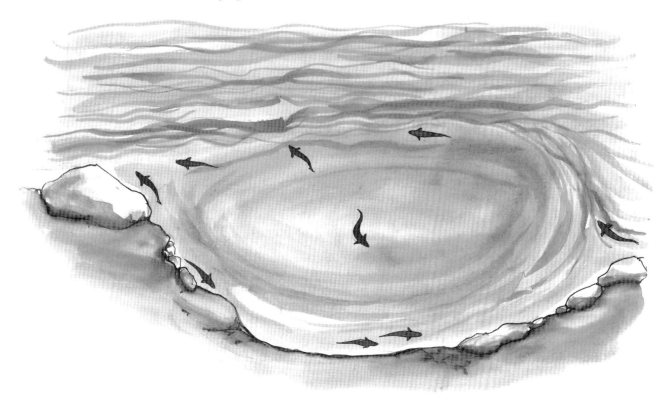

Trout may hold in various areas of an eddy, so it is helpful to stop and watch for fish movement before you start casting.

Eddies form where obstructions and the shape of the bank create a circular flow.

Areas where the depth changes from shallow to deep often hold trout.

Depressions on the stream bottom create pockets of slow water where trout can get out of the current and still be close to food.

provide good cover from predators, trout sometimes swim below foam for safety, then make occasional forays into other parts of the eddy for a quick meal. Drifting a nymph under or near the foam is an excellent way to catch some nice fish. Over the years, I have caught some of my largest trout from eddies.

Changes in Depth. Changes in depth can occur at various locations in a stream. Obstructions in the current such as logs or boulders often cause current deflections that erode the substrate and create holes or deeper slots along the stream bottom. Whenever the direction of the current changes, there are often shear forces that also change the bottom profile and thus the depth of the water. These changes create areas along the stream bottom with slower current than the water a foot or two above. Trout sit in the slow water along the bottom and swim up into the faster water above to feed on food drifting overhead.

Changes in Current Speed. This refers to areas where different current speeds flow next to each other. Though various structures can cause this, it commonly occurs where a riffle forms at a river bend. The inside corner of the bend usually has slow water along the edge of the faster riffle. Such corners typically get scoured during

The edges between fast and slow water concentrate food and attract feeding trout.

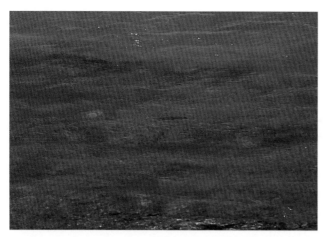

Lush beds of aquatic plants often harbor large numbers of aquatic insects and provide good habitat for trout.

high flows, so they contain differences in water depth as well. Trout like to hang out in the slower, deeper water at the corner of the riffle and can easily move into the faster water to feed if needed. The result is a hot spot perfect for fishing with nymphs, since nymphs and larvae make up most of the food drifting along the bottom of the riffle.

Aquatic Plants. Aquatic plants, especially rooted ones, generally occur where currents are moderate to slow and fine sediment has accumulated on the bottom. They generally do not grow in deep water, because they need plenty of sunlight. Their habitat is spotty in most streams and rivers, so aquatic plants typically occur in patches. Streams with more slow water and fine sediment have larger and more frequent patches of plants than streams with fast water and a rocky bottom. Beds of aquatic plants attract trout because they can hide from predators among the leaves and stems, the plants slow the current, and aquatic insects live on the stems and leaves, resulting in a plentiful food supply. It can be difficult to fish subsurface flies directly over beds of aquatic plants, as the flies frequently snag the vegetation. Fishing in gaps between beds of aquatic plants or along their edges can be an effective tactic, however.

Pools. Pools, areas where the channel deepens and the current slows, come in all shapes and sizes, depending on the type of stream or river you're fishing. The importance of pools varies with the type of stream and the amount of food and cover they provide trout. Pools give shelter from fast current, and the deeper water provides protection from some predators. But predators that swim, such as otters and mergansers, may actually find catching fish easier in these areas. Pools with wood debris or logs offer better protection.

An important factor affecting how many trout a particular pool will hold is how much food is available in the pool. Large, slow pools with sandy bottoms and little vegetation along the shore provide little food and will not hold many trout. The exception might be migrating fish. During spawning migrations, salmon and trout don't feed, and their main need is a place to rest. Large pools provide perfect resting spots. For nonspawning fish, however, pools need to provide food as well as slow water and cover to be hot spots.

Food enters pools either from above, when adult aquatic or terrestrial insects land on the water, or from below, when nymphs and larvae drift into the pool from faster water upstream. Therefore, when surface food is not plentiful, the majority of food will be at the head or upstream end, where faster water flows into the pool, and nymph fishing will be most effective there as well.

Recognizing Hot Spots

One of the challenges anglers face is learning to recognize likely hot spots under different conditions and in different types of streams. Exactly what kind of hot spots you will find and where they occur in streams depend on many factors. One of the main factors is simply the size of the stream. A large river will have quite different habitat

Trout may hold in various locations of a pool, depending on their activity and the stream flow. Most active feeding generally occurs at the head (front) and tail (rear) of the pool. The deepest part provides good cover and protection.

Rafting is quite popular on many large rivers.

characteristics than a small creek. The key needs of the trout are the same and the kinds of structure creating habitat are similar, but the types and locations of hot spots will be different. To help you learn to recognize hot spots in different kinds of waterways, I have divided the world of rivers and streams into four categories: large rivers, medium streams, small streams, and spring creeks. The reality, of course, is that there are many variations. But if you can recognize the basic types of hot spots within each of these categories, you will increase your chances of catching trout in all types of moving water.

Large Rivers. I consider a river large when it is big enough to easily float in a boat or raft and too big to wade across. The western part of North America has many such large rivers. The Midwest and East also have large rivers, but they are fewer in number, especially if one considers only trout streams. My home river, the Deschutes, is a large river, at least along its lower one hundred miles. Like any river, it becomes smaller upstream, changing gradually to a medium stream and then to a small stream near its source.

If you don't routinely fish large rivers, you might feel intimidated by their size when you do fish them. The large expanse of water seems to create so many choices about where to fish that confusion can set in. Plus, casting a size 18 nymph into a river two hundred feet wide can seem like a fruitless endeavor. But if you learn to recognize the hot spots on large rivers, you can narrow your casting down to the most productive areas.

Bank water. You can greatly simplify fishing large rivers by ignoring most of the water. Focus your attention only on the area near each bank by considering the area from the shore out ten or twenty feet on either side as a separate small stream. Look carefully, just within this zone, for prime trout lies or hot spots. Identify boulders and small eddies along the bank where trout might hold, paying special attention to areas where foam lines form. Look for undercut banks and overhanging vegetation that provide cover and food. In many cases, the area within ten or twenty feet of a large river's shore provides numerous hot spots and holds a lot of trout, and by focusing your attention on a smaller area, reading the water becomes much less confusing.

Riffle tailouts. The tailouts of riffles, areas where they end, typically produce distinct changes in depth and current velocity. The best riffle tailouts generally occur where the river channel makes a slight turn, producing slower, deeper areas on the inside of the corner. The result is prime holding areas for trout and excellent conditions for nymphing. Look carefully where the breaks in depth and velocity occur, and focus your fishing along those edges or seams.

Focusing your attention along the banks can make a large river feel less confusing or overwhelming.

Always stop and take a close look for fish in eddies along the banks of large rivers and any size stream. Note the foam lines above this trout and farther out in the water.

Pocket water. Long riffles punctuated with boulders produce classic pocket water conditions. The most fishable pocket water tends to occur in medium streams, where the depths and velocities are not as great as in large rivers. In large rivers, wade such areas with caution. Here you may be able to wade and fish only along the edges of the riffles and associated pocket water. A wading staff can be a valuable tool when fishing fast-water areas in a large river.

Runs. Runs in large rivers are rather fast and deep, four to eight feet, with boulders sprinkled along the bottom. This makes them difficult places to wade and fish, though good trout will hold along the bottom where boulders break the main force of the current. Sinking lines and heavy flies usually are needed to fish such areas successfully.

Flats. Many large rivers have long flats where the water moves relatively slowly, the surface remains calm, and the depth is moderate, (two to six feet deep). Excellent dry-fly fishing often occurs on flats when adult insects are abundant. Nymph fishing can also be productive when trout focus their feeding during a hatch below the surface on rising nymphs or pupae. Look for areas where bottom depressions, boulders, or beds of aquatic plants provide trout cover and slower current.

Pools. In large rivers, pools can be quite deep, more than ten feet, and two hundred to three hundred feet long. Though trout will hold in these big pools, it is difficult to know where they may be hiding unless distinct structure is present. There is less food in large pools than in other parts of the river, so trout in pools often do not feed aggressively. For these reasons, I rarely fish pools in large rivers unless I see trout feeding.

Eddies. Eddies are one of my favorite habitats to fish on large rivers. They often form where the channel makes a sharp turn or large obstructions such as a downed tree or group of boulders jut out from shore. In large rivers, eddies may be forty or fifty feet across. The large area of circling current traps a wide variety of food, both surface and subsurface, for trout to eat. Perhaps the biggest challenge when fishing such large eddies is getting your fly to drift naturally to the fish. The conflicting current directions can quickly introduce drag, which generally puts fish off. Use a longer leader than normal, mend frequently, and be patient. Before casting, watch the eddy carefully for signs of feeding fish. Spotting the location of fish within the eddy can greatly improve your chances of a hookup.

The area below riffles where the water deepens and slows provides some of the best nymphing water on larger rivers.

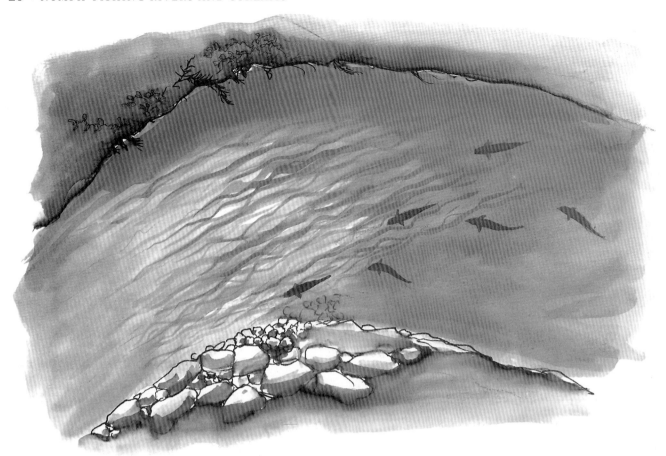

Trout take advantage of the changes in depth and velocity where riffle tailouts occur.

The pockets of slow water behind boulders are good places to explore with nymphs and drys.

Flats often produce good hatches and surface action, but make sure fish aren't feeding on rising nymphs or pupae below the surface before you start fishing dry flies.

Runs are great places to fish nymphs, but you need enough weight to get them near the bottom.

Wood debris in large rivers tends to be anchored along the shore where strong currents can't wash it away.

Logs and wood. Because of the volume of water in large rivers, logs and wood debris have a hard time staying put and often get washed downstream. Logs also may be removed on purpose if the river is used for commercial boat traffic. As a result, logs and large pieces of wood do not produce instream habitat as commonly on large rivers as they do on medium streams or small streams. In most cases, the best conditions for wood debris or logs on large rivers occur along the bank where they get caught or trapped partly in and partly out of the water.

Medium Streams. I think of medium-size streams as those that you cannot easily float in a boat or raft during summer flows and can wade across from one bank to the other at only a few locations. Pools and runs on medium streams are too deep to wade across, but shallow riffle areas can generally be crossed. Medium-size streams provide nearly ideal conditions for fly fishing. They are small enough to wade safely to within casting distance of most hot spots, they provide a good mix of habitat types for trout to live in, and I feel as though I have a more intimate connection with the stream than I do on a large river. Many of the hot spots on a medium stream are similar to those on a large river, but they are often easier to distinguish and fish.

Bank water. A complete range of bank conditions occurs on medium streams. In some areas, undercut banks may be common. Along other banks, boulders may create small eddies and excellent holding water for trout to sip nymphs below the surface and terrestrial insects on top. Just as you should on large rivers, carefully study and assess banks on medium streams before wading out into the water to fish. Some of the best trout in the stream often are just a foot or two from shore.

Riffle tailouts. Riffles on medium streams are generally shorter and less violent than those on large rivers. This usually translates into more fishable water. Pay close attention to riffle tailouts and any area where changes in depth and velocity occur. Trout especially seek out riffles and riffle tailouts during the summer and early fall, when water temperatures rise and oxygen levels drop in many streams. The surface agitation in riffles reoxygenates the water, providing trout a breath of fresh air.

Pocket water. After you are done fishing a riffle tailout, move up into the riffle and fish the pocket water. The lower flows and velocities found in medium streams make wading safer and the pockets found around boulders more accessible. It is also easier to get a nymph down to the fish in the lower velocities of medium streams.

In medium-size streams, you can often approach banks from the middle of the stream. Banks like this, with overhanging trees and logs, provide excellent cover and habitat.

The banks along streams without large trees and wood are still important and attract trout.

The inside corner of a riffle tailout typically provides an area of slow water next to swift currents. This is always a good area to explore with nymphs.

Boulders produce great pocket water that you can explore with nymphs or dry flies.

In medium-size streams, the added depth of runs attracts many trout.

Flats need to be approached carefully to avoid spooking fish even when casting nymphs.

Trout sometimes cruise through pools looking for tasty insects in the surface or near the bottom. Watch carefully to determine where to present your fly.

Eddies trap food and attract trout.

Large pieces of wood lying in the stream channel provide cover and slow-water habitats that almost always hold a few trout.

Runs. Runs can be excellent places to fish nymphs in medium-size streams. Trout often stay right off the bottom in runs, avoiding the main force of the current by sitting behind large rocks or boulders. A large number of nymphs and larvae also live in runs. You can take a lot of fish by drifting a nymph directly off the bottom.

Flats. Flats tend to become important during good hatches. Adult insects floating on the quiet surface are like sitting ducks to hungry trout. During a hatch, most fly fishers begin with dry flies. Though drys often work, there are times when trout appear to be taking adults but are actually taking emerging nymphs or pupae just below the surface. This is when you should fish subsurface nymphs and emergers. You need a quiet approach and gentle presentation, or you will see just how fast trout can disappear.

Pools. Pools become more fishable in medium streams. Those with good structure, such as logs, boulders, or root wads, hold more fish than open pools with little cover. The faster water at the head or upstream end carries nymphs and larvae into the pool, creating an excellent place to fish nymphs.

Eddies. Large eddies are not as common on medium streams as they are on large rivers. Instead, you likely will find eddies from a few feet to perhaps ten feet in diameter. Even though they look small, don't pass them by without careful observation. I've caught some very nice fish out of eddies no bigger around than a basketball. Foam swirling on the surface makes it harder to see fish, but it also seems to attract fish. Pay close attention to areas where foam has formed.

Logs and wood. Logs and large pieces of wood commonly provide excellent habitat for trout in medium streams. Sometimes the wood may span the entire channel; other times a log resting on shore and angled into the stream forms a perfect hiding and feeding spot for a large trout. Brown trout are especially fond of areas with dense cover created by wood and logs.

Small Streams. Small streams or creeks make up the majority of stream miles in any watershed or basin. They don't attract as much attention from anglers, because in most cases, trout don't grow as large in small streams as they do in large or medium-size rivers. Small streams may be just a few feet wide or up to thirty feet across. They are too small to float, and you can easily wade across them at shallow riffles and often through pools. Though small streams may not routinely grow large trout, they often have complex structure and habitat that can hold good numbers of fish.

One of the things I like most about small streams is the intimate connection I feel with them. You are within a few feet of each nook and cranny that might hold a trout, and you quickly see whether your cast caused a trout to take your fly or spooked it downstream. Perhaps the biggest challenge on small streams is keeping your fly out of overhanging branches and tree limbs. When I first started fishing them, it felt as if every tree or shrub along the bank wanted to reach out and grab my fly. Using short rods (7–8 ft.) and shorter leaders (6–7 ft.) can greatly reduce this problem. And practice, practice, practice. The line control lessons you learn on a small stream will also serve you well on larger rivers.

Bank water. Every bit of useful habitat is important to the fish in small streams. Banks are no exception. Because of the modest amount of water in small streams, a critical factor in most habitats is water depth. Water over three feet deep may be rare in many small streams. Banks on the outside of a bend in the stream channel may have some of the deepest water in the stream. This depth alone attracts trout. If the bank has good cover from overhanging shrubs or trees or is slightly undercut, all the better. Some of the best bank conditions I've found on small streams occur when water has eroded the soil away from the roots of a tree, leaving the tree standing half in and half out of the water. The area under and around the roots creates a wonderful tangle that's a perfect shelter for trout. Don't try to drift a fly back under the tangle, but a fly drifted along the edge of the roots will often entice a hungry trout to come out for a quick snack.

Riffle tailouts. Most riffles in a small stream are too shallow to hold many fish. The tailouts of riffles, however, usually create deeper water. This is where you want to drift a nymph. Look for the deepest slots and channels where rocks or boulders deflect the current. These almost always hold the nicest fish.

Pocket water. Pocket water can be found anywhere a boulder big enough to create slack water behind it occurs. In small streams, it may be better to search this water with a dry fly than a nymph, but if you aren't getting any action on the surface, try drifting a juicy stonefly or caddisfly nymph downstream along the edge of the boulder and into the slack water behind it.

Runs. Sometimes it's hard to tell where a riffle stops and a run begins on a small stream. That's because the depths and velocities don't change as radically between riffles and runs in a small stream as they do in medium or large rivers. In small streams, a run may simply be a short, deep section between two pools. I like to look for those with rocks or debris, which provides trout some shelter from the current.

Flats. Flats are not a dominant habitat in small streams, because they are generally small and so shallow that trout feel too vulnerable to hang out there. The tailouts of pools provide most of the flats like fishing conditions in small streams.

Blown-down trees along the banks of small streams provide areas with deeper water and good cover for trout.

Riffle tailouts in small streams often drop into pools. Areas where the water deepens and slow and fast water meet can be excellent places to fish with nymphs.

You often have to take turns fishing pocket water and other habitat in small streams.

The tailouts of pools produce typical flats in many small streams.

The head of a pool is a good place to cast a nymph in a small stream.

Large pieces of wood produce some of the best habitat available to trout when they fall into the channels of small streams.

Pools. Because deep water is in such limited supply in small streams, pools provide some of the most important habitat. Both the head or upstream end of the pool and the tail or bottom of the pool should be fished carefully. The faster water flowing into the head of the pool carries in nymphs from upstream and thus provides the best conditions for fishing a nymph. At the tail of the pool, I prefer to fish a dry fly, often a beetle or ant pattern. The biggest trout in a small stream are often found at the head of a large pool where rocks or wood provide good cover.

Eddies. Eddies are a less frequent habitat feature in small streams than in medium or large rivers. Where they occur, they still trap food, provide relief from the current, and attract trout. In small streams, eddies are often just a foot or two in diameter, tucked behind a boulder or log.

Logs and wood. Logs and large pieces of wood can be very important in small streams. In fact, in forested areas, wood is one of the primary factors that create good fish habitat in small streams. Logs and wood slow the current, creating pools and needed deep water; divert the flow into side channels, forming more complex stream channels and habitat diversity; and provide excellent cover. In open prairie or rangeland areas, there may be little wood available to fall into the stream, but where it does fall, it provides excellent cover and habitat for trout.

One of the best sources for wood in small streams comes from our furry friend the beaver. Beaver dams create diverse habitat and more consistent flows downstream, and the large beaver ponds above the dams provide excellent habitat for trout. One of the first major environmental impacts Europeans had on North American trout streams was trapping out most of the beavers.

Spring Creeks. Spring creeks are the crown jewels of trout streams. Like rare gems, they form only where the right conditions occur. Most streams and rivers form from a network of tiny intermittent channels that coalesce with other channels until enough come together to form a small perennial stream, and then enough small streams come together to create a medium stream, and then enough medium streams flow together to create a large river, and so on until you are floating down the Hudson or Mississippi or Columbia River. Spring creeks, however, usually begin full-blown at a relatively defined point where either one large spring or numerous small ones burst forth from the ground with enough water to create a stream. These springs often deliver water from deep underground aquifers that produce water at a constant flow and temperature throughout the year. And because spring creeks begin at such a defined spot, they have no upstream channels delivering dirt, wood, or runoff from

The beginning of a spring creek.

natural or human disturbances. This accounts for the crystalline quality of most spring creeks. The first time I stepped into one to fish, I thought the creek was no more than a foot deep, when suddenly I found myself in four feet of water—about six inches above the tops of my hip boots. Near constant flow and temperature also result in unique conditions for aquatic plants, insects, and trout.

Spring creeks come in many sizes, but most fall into the small or medium category. Though there are exceptions, most flow at a gentle pace owing to the gentle tilt of the land they flow across and the modest amount of water in their channels. Trout find conditions in springs creeks much to their liking. Gentle currents, near constant flow, plenty of food, and temperatures that hover around 50 degrees F in summer and winter mean trout eat and grow at a near constant rate all year long. In a sense, spring creeks are to trout what South Pacific islands are to people: perfect weather, lots of food that's easy to collect, and little need to work—in short, paradise. As a result, spring creeks often produce trout much larger than you would find in free-flowing streams of similar size.

The best fishing spots in spring creeks don't always compare with hot spots in other streams or rivers. Because the water is so clear, trout quickly learn that they have to hide to survive. Thus they stick close to cover. In

Crystal-clear water and gentle currents typify most spring creeks.

spring creeks, aquatic plants form some of the best cover. Look for trout tucked behind patches of plants or in small, open channels between thick plant beds. The plant beds contain numerous insects for food, and when frightened, trout can quickly dive into the plants for safety. Other features, such as undercut banks, logs and wood debris, and boulders, still provide prime habitat for trout in spring creeks.

You can improve your success in spring creeks by spotting and fishing to individual trout. This isn't difficult when they are rising at the surface, but for fishing nymphs, you must develop an eye for spotting trout along the bottom.

In this spring creek, like many others, wood and aquatic vegetation provide the cover and food trout need.

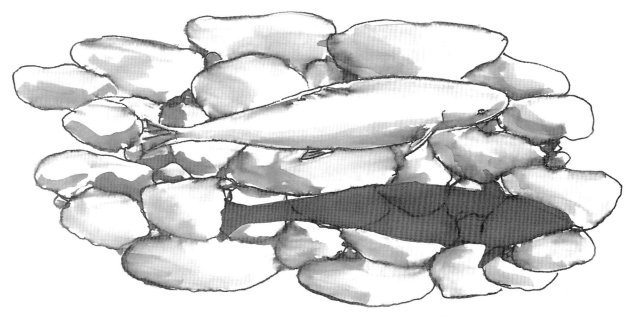

Trout are incredibly well camouflaged, but they have a hard time hiding their shadows.

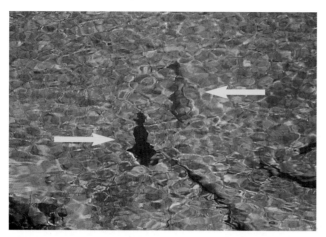

The trout (arrow, above right) *is almost invisible, but its shadow* (arrow, lower left) *stands out and can be easily seen.*

Fly fishing and fly fishermen would have evolved quite differently if insects didn't drift and trout weren't drift feeders.

This is easier said than done and takes practice to perfect. One secret is not to look for a fish, but for the shadow of a fish on the stream bottom. The color of trout blends in with the surroundings incredibly well, but a shadow is hard to camouflage. Once you see the shadow, check the direction of the sun so you can visually backtrack to where the trout should be. The possibility of spotting individual fish is one reason fishing spring creeks is so interesting and exciting. Remember, trout in spring creeks are quite skittish and easily spooked by clumsy wading, a cast that lands with a splash, or a fly that moves unnaturally.

Trout Feeding Behavior

Fortunately for fly fishers, insect behavior and fish feeding behavior, especially that of trout, have evolved to provide the perfect opportunity for fooling fish with artificial flies. This may seem obvious, but the details are sometimes complex and always helpful to understand if you want to be more successful.

When you watch trout underwater in their natural habitat, you quickly realize how perfectly suited they are to their environment. The fish seems to hold still in the current without any effort. A tiny flick of the tail, a little turn of a pectoral fin is all it takes for it to adjust to the continual movement of the current. Then, faster than you can blink, it darts a foot to the right or left, or up or down, then effortlessly glides back to the original spot. It usually happens so fast that you can't see what fins the fish moved to propel itself like a bionic dart, but this is what makes trout the perfect quarry for fly fishers—because trout, more than any other freshwater fish, concentrate their feeding on what's drifting in or on the water. This means an artificial fly drifting in the current has at least a chance of looking like food to them.

Imagine what fly fishing would be like if trout had evolved to feed only on food attached to the bottom. Instead of casting a size 16 caddis pupa with a 3-weight fly rod, you'd be lobbing a snail imitation with enough weight to sink it like a rock to the bottom. A heavy casting rod would perform this better than a fly rod, and instead of wading in the stream, you'd be sitting in a lounge chair with a beer propped on your belly. We should definitely give thanks that trout have turned to what drifts in the current as their main source of food.

Trout have lived up to their half of the equation by becoming drift feeders. The other half of the story is about what's drifting for them to eat. Most of the time the answer is simple: aquatic insects. Therefore, we need to look closely at insect drift and what it means to nymph fishing.

Aquatic insects have all the basic needs of any animal: food, shelter, protection from predators, and reproduction. Now imagine the difficulties of meeting these needs for organisms as small as aquatic insects in an environment as dynamic as streams and rivers. How do they find new sources of food, minimize competition for food, avoid predators, and find the right habitats to live in? On land, insects can take off across the ground with relative ease or, with their wings, cover large distances rather quickly. But how does a tiny insect move against a strong current? Though aquatic insects are well adapted to live with the current, moving upstream against it would be like driving the wrong direction on a freeway at rush hour. The solution, as any good Zen master would tell you, is simple: Don't struggle against the force of the current; let go and drift with it. And thus insect drift was born.

Insect Drift Activity

The common, everyday type of drift activity is called behavioral drift. A less frequent and irregular form called catastrophic drift occurs in response to extreme changes in the environment, such as floods, droughts, or chemical spills. Catastrophic drift is like a stampeding herd of cattle running away from a tornado. Behavioral drift is like the daily movement of deer or elk for feeding and sleeping, with the distinction that the movement of aquatic insects occurs in only one direction—downstream. For feeding trout and nymph-fishing anglers, behavioral drift is of key importance.

There have been numerous studies of behavioral drift, and they have uncovered many interesting and useful facts. Some level of drift occurs all the time, but there are periods of the day when drift activity peaks, and these peaks occur at three well-defined times over a twenty-four-hour period. The first peak is in the morning, generally starting an hour before and ending roughly an hour after sunrise. The second peak is in the evening, lasting from about an hour before to an hour after sunset. The third peak occurs in the middle of the night, from around midnight to 2 A.M. These periods of peak drift activity occur consistently every day throughout the year, though the intensity of the peaks may vary from day to day with changes in weather, water temperature, and stream flows. The obvious importance to fly fishers is that periods of peak drift are when more food is available to trout, which respond by increasing their feeding activity. It has long been known that fishing success tends to be high early and late in the day, and the peaks in insect drift at these times is one possible reason.

Some insect species are much more common in the drift than others. This makes sense, given that some species are much more active and mobile than others. Stone-cased caddis larvae, for example, are not likely to drift far in the current. On the other hand, species that swim well, like blue-winged olive mayflies (*Baetis* sp.), often end up in the drift. If you know what insects are the most frequent drifters, you will know what fly patterns to

Major types of insect drift

- **Catastrophic drift.** Occurs only when floods, droughts, or chemical spills occur and force insects to escape an area.
- **Behaviorial drift.** A daily activity used by many aquatic insects to find new uncrowded habitats and avoid predators.
- **Emergence drift.** Occurs when mature nymphs or pupae leave the stream bottom and drift to the surface for adult emergence.
- **Surface drift.** Occurs when adult insects emerge on the surface and when they return to lay eggs.

use when fishing during periods of peak drift activity. A simple example of actual drift data from a small coastal stream in Oregon shows how the tendency to drift varies among species.

Insect	Percent of total insects collected in the drift
Mayfly *(Baetis)*	18%
Mayfly *(Centroptilum)*	3%
Mayfly *(Paraleptophlebia)*	2%
Stonefly *(Sweltsa)*	2%
Stonefly *(Calineuria californica)*	1%
Diptera (Chironomidae larvae)	29%
Diptera (Chironomidae pupae)	6%
Diptera (Chironomidae adults)	6%
Water mites	7%
Copepods	7%

Behavioral drift of nymphs and larvae along the stream bottom is a key reason why nymph fishing is so successful.

In this example, it is pretty clear that *Baetis* and chironomid (midge) larvae are the most abundant insects in the drift. A drift study on the South Fork of the Boise River in Idaho, found chironomid larvae and *Baetis* and *Ephemerella* (mayfly) nymphs to be the most abundant. Other species often found to be abundant in the drift include certain caddisflies, such as *Hydropsyche* (net-spinning caddis) and *Brachycentrus* (American Grannon caddis), and amphipods or scuds. Stonefly nymphs are generally not as common. Many species of aquatic insects drift, but studies consistently show blue-winged olives and chironomids at or near the top of the list of the most abundant drifters. Because *Baetis* and chironomids are so abundant in most trout streams and tend to dominate the insects in the drift during daily behavioral drift periods, fly patterns that match them are excellent choices when fishing early or late in the day and no other insect activity is obvious.

The next factor that affects drift is adult emergence. Most aquatic insect nymphs and larvae live on the stream bottom, clinging to the substrate. Most adult emergence, however, occurs at the water's surface. Thus, when ready for adult emergence, mature nymphs or pupae must let go of the stream bottom and swim or float to the surface. From the time they leave the bottom until they reach the surface, they are drifting downstream. How far they drift depends on the current speed and their ability to swim. Even nymphs that crawl out on the bank for adult emergence, such as stoneflies, must crawl across the stream bottom to reach the bank. This increases their exposure to the currents and thus the number drifting.

Emergence drift is tied to periods of adult emergence and thus does not occur at the same time of the day throughout the year like behavioral drift. During cool periods of the year—fall, winter, and spring—most emergence activity takes place during the warmest part of the day, typically 11 A.M. to 3 P.M. During the summer, emergence activity is usually concentrated in the morning or evening or, for a few species, at night. Emergence drift is not dominated by the same consistent species as is behavioral drift. Instead, it is dominated by whatever species is emerging at the time. Choosing the right pattern for emergence drift depends on recognizing what adults are emerging and knowing what their nymphs or pupae look like drifting in the current. A great variety of emerging nymph and pupa patterns have been developed just for this purpose.

Another type of drift, surface drift, is most important to fly fishers who use only dry flies. The other forms of drift occur underwater. Anglers may be unaware of them for that reason, but they are very important, since trout usually feed on what's drifting below the surface. But fortunately for those who sell expensive rooster hackles, trout also feed on insects drifting on the surface of the water. Interestingly, some fly fishers have reached the conclusion that only surface feeding is worthy of the fly fisher's skill and art, and anything fished below the surface is beneath them. Though this makes no sense biologically, it

Nymphs and pupae rising to the surface for adult emergence produces another important period of subsurface drift on which trout feed heavily.

has made for interesting philosophical debates between dry-fly purists and those who fish wet flies and nymphs.

Three different situations create surface drift. The first is emerging adults. Once drifting nymphs or pupae reach the surface, newly emerged adults sit on the water's surface for a few seconds to a minute or more before flying off. During that time, they drift a few feet to hundreds of feet, providing fish—and anglers—something to get excited about. Surface drift activity also occurs when adult aquatic insects return to lay their eggs, usually a few days to a few weeks after emergence. Most aquatic adults lay their eggs on the water's surface, drifting with the current while releasing their eggs. Many then die on the surface and continue drifting. As a result, adult egg-laying activity provides another excellent opportunity for fishing dry flies. The third form of surface drift occurs when terrestrial insects fall onto the surface of the water. Most terrestrials float and struggle in the water's surface until they reach shore and the safety of dry land or a hungry trout zeros in on their helpless flailing. Warm summer afternoons with a moderate breeze provide the greatest opportunities for this type of surface drift, although any time terrestrials are near water, they frequently end up as fish food.

Surface drift activity does not occur at consistent intervals like behavioral drift. It is subject to a variety of factors that control emergence and egg-laying behavior and terrestrial insect activity. Weather and time of year have the greatest influence, but many other factors also play a role. Because surface drift is not hidden beneath the surface like the other forms of drift, careful observation of what's on the surface and how fish are feeding will tell you when, where, and what to fish.

Influences on Food Choices

With all these forms of insect drift, it is obvious that trout have a number of options when it comes to feeding. They need to decide not only what to feed on, but also when to feed. Several factors influence their choices.

Food Abundance. Because trout have to use energy efficiently, they feed most heavily when the greatest amount of food is present. Going to the grocery store when the shelves are nearly bare is a waste of time and energy that most wild creatures, including trout, can't afford to make. There are times of the day when food is naturally more abundant. Mornings and evenings are almost always such times. Another key period of abundant food is when large numbers of nymphs or pupae are drifting prior to adult emergence. Food also becomes more abundant when aquatic adults are emerging or laying eggs on the surface or when terrestrial insects fall into the water. Thus trout feeding behavior clearly is directly linked to insect behavior.

Cloudy, overcast days are usually good times to catch trout.

Light Conditions. The light conditions—whether the day is sunny and bright or cloudy and dark—can affect trout and insect behavior. Fish have no eyelids to shade their eyes from bright light, so on a sunny day, they are less likely to stay out in the open, preferring instead to rest in the shade of streamside trees or stay in deeper water where the harsh sunlight has been filtered a bit through the water. It doesn't mean you won't find trout in areas exposed to the sun, but they spend less time in such places and are often more easily spooked. On cloudy, overcast days, trout often are more active and spend more time in areas open to the sky as long as the food supply is adequate.

Insects are affected in much the same way. On bright, sunny days, insect hatches are often suppressed or concentrated into a narrow period of time, say one or two hours. On cloudy days, hatches are usually heavier and last longer, often extending over three or four hours. Insect drift may also be more abundant on overcast days than on sunny ones, and the drift periods in the morning and evening often last longer on overcast days. I never turn down a chance to fish on a sunny day, mind you, but I do try to fish in shady areas and don't expect trout to feed as heavily or for as long.

Weather. Weather and light conditions go somewhat hand in hand, as sunny days usually occur during periods of high pressure and cloudy days during periods of low pressure. I've met some anglers who feel that fishing is always best during a low-pressure system. I have also met anglers who feel it is best during a high-pressure system. I have experienced good and bad days of fishing under both scenarios and find it hard to conclude that one produces better fishing than the other.

More than high or low pressure, I think a downturn in fish feeding activity often occurs when a front is approaching and the barometric pressure changes quickly either up or down. The bigger the change in barometric pressure, the bigger the apparent effect on the fish. Big changes in barometric pressure also tend to produce rather unsettled weather conditions, such as strong wind, hard rain, or hail, and such conditions turn off a lot of the insect activity and make the simple act of casting a difficult prospect. The result is usually pretty poor fishing. The nice thing about fishing, however, is that anyone who has fished for a while will have stories that contradict such statements.

Water Temperature. Fish are cold-blooded animals. This is not a personality trait, but a reference to their body temperature, which is the same temperature as the water they inhabit. Temperature affects all animals, but for cold-blooded animals, it directly affects all aspects of their life: feeding, growth, reproduction, and general survival.

Trout, salmon, and char—essentially all the fish in the family Salmonidae—are referred to as cold-water fish because they thrive best in cold water. In contrast, bass, walleye, and catfish are called warm-water fish because they thrive in warm water.

How cold is cold and how warm is warm, and what is the ideal temperature for a species? These questions have been asked and studied by hundreds of fish biologists over many years. One thing all this research has discovered is that there is no single answer. Different salmonids have slightly different temperature preferences, and even individuals of the same species show different temperature preferences in different regions where they live. This reflects the ability of a species to adapt or evolve to local conditions—within certain limits. Most trout species find water temperatures from 50 to 60 degrees F ideal. Species that have evolved in the far north, such as arctic char and bull trout, prefer lower temperatures of 40 to 50 degrees. The desert red-band trout, a subspecies of rainbow, has evolved in warm desert streams and not only tolerates

but will continue to grow in streams that reach 80 degrees during the summer.

In addition to basic survival, temperature also affects feeding behavior. The cold-blooded nature of fish means that their metabolism is linked to the water temperature. When water temperature drops below their preferred temperature range, their metabolism also drops and feeding activity declines. It doesn't stop, and thus you can still catch trout in the middle of the winter, but you won't find them feeding as frequently or aggressively as during the summer. When the water temperature rises above their preferred range, their metabolism continues to increase, but feeding may actually slow down as a result of stress from the warm water.

The best way to use this information in your everyday fishing is to track how the temperature in the stream or river changes throughout the day. No matter what the time of year, the water temperature will vary from early morning to early evening by several degrees, unless you are fishing a spring creek that flows at a constant temperature. Increased feeding activity usually occurs at the time of day when the temperature falls in or closest to the preferred temperature range of the fish. During warm summer weather, this generally means early to midmorning or late evening. In the winter, it means midday will produce the greatest feeding activity. A heavy hatch or large egg-laying flight of adult insects can still trigger heavy feeding during less ideal temperature periods, but as temperatures move farther and farther from the preferred range, even a heavy hatch may go untouched.

Temperature also affects how much stress a fish experiences from being caught. In warm water, which holds less dissolved oxygen than does cold water, not only are fish feeling stressed from the high water temperature, but when they exercise hard, such as when fighting at the end of your line, they run short of oxygen just as we do when exercising at high altitudes. For most trout, when water temperatures are over 70 degrees F, you should play them quickly and rest them carefully in the water before releasing them. At temperatures over 75 degrees, you might consider not even fishing for trout because of the possibility of killing fish you catch, especially if on a stream where such warm temperatures are rare. Cold temperatures don't pose the same kinds of problems, but you may need to give trout more time to recover by holding them gently in a slight current before releasing them when temperatures are in the thirties or forties.

Time of Day and Time of Year. Daily and seasonal feeding rhythms are primarily driven by the factors described above. For example, increased feeding activity routinely coincides with peak behavioral drift cycles in the morning and evening and during increased drift related to adult emergence or egg laying. Seasonal weather conditions tend to push adult insect activity from midday during cold weather in the late fall, winter, and early spring to mid-morning or evening in the warmer months of late spring, summer, and early fall. Finally, major changes in the weather can alter feeding patterns rather unpredictably at any time of year.

Selective Feeding

A discussion of feeding behavior wouldn't be complete without some mention of selective versus nonselective feeding. What causes selective feeding, when does it occur, and does it matter when fishing nymphs? If you've been fly-fishing for long, you've probably noticed that trout in some streams feed quite selectively and seem to have amazing "stream smarts" when it comes to distinguishing fake flies from the real thing, while in other streams trout seem quite gullible, even downright stupid. On heavily fished catch-and-release streams, the theory goes, trout learn to recognize artificial flies, the leader, and unnatural drag from all the conditioning they get over the course of a fishing season. This may be part of the answer, but selective versus nonselective feeding goes beyond how many times a fish gets caught or sees artificial flies. But first let me be clear about what I mean by selectivity.

Selective feeding means that fish focus all their feeding on one specific type of food to the exclusion of other foods that may be just as available. In some cases, the food selected isn't even the most abundant. Why? First, selective feeding almost always occurs in productive waters that have a high abundance of available food. In waters like this, where finding food isn't the main problem, going after every different type of food can actually use more energy than focusing attention on one single abundant type of food and feeding on it exclusively. Thus when blue-winged olive nymphs drift in large numbers or a mass of green rock worm caddis pupae begin swimming to the surface to emerge, it saves trout energy to feed selectively on this single abundant food. Plus, when trout get caught numerous times on heavily fished waters, they also learn to pay closer attention to unusual characteristics of their food, such as leaders or drag. All of a sudden, these fish become much harder to fool and seem much smarter than your average trout.

On waters with low productivity and therefore a limited food supply for fish, and in remote areas where trout rarely see an angler, such as many streams in Alaska, feeding behavior is different. In waters where food is scarce, trout can't afford to be choosy and will sample anything that drifts by that looks like something to eat. If it isn't food, they simply spit it out and try the next likely looking item in the drift. And if the fish have never been caught or seen an artificial fly with a leader attached, then they won't associate it with something unpleasant. These trout aren't selective or cautious. As a result, they are relatively easy to catch and may even seem stupid in their eagerness to grab your fly.

I find it interesting that people aren't all that different when it comes to selectivity. If you're at a party with dozens of different desserts to choose from after eating a large meal, you will likely be rather selective about which one you pick. But if you've been on a long backpacking trip with nothing to eat but freeze-dried food for several weeks, and then arrive at a party with only two or three desserts to choose from and not enough for everyone, you will probably grab the first dessert you see and not spend much time analyzing it before gobbling it up. Selectivity seems more a matter of circumstance than intelligence.

There is a common belief among many anglers that brown trout are hard to catch and therefore smart, whereas cutthroat trout are easy to catch and therefore stupid. But look at the environments in which these two species live: Brown trout most frequently inhabit moderate to large, slightly warmer, and usually highly productive streams and rivers; cutthroat trout often live in moderate to small streams at higher altitudes, which are cold and less productive. These conditions put brown trout in areas where it pays to be selective and cutthroats in areas where it pays to be nonselective. I have come across cutthroat trout in productive streams during heavy hatches that have rivaled brown trout in selectivity and difficulty to catch. Any species feeding behavior is shaped to a large degree by the environment in which it lives.

When fish become selective, how do they decide what is and what isn't on their menu? One theory I like explains that selectively feeding fish create a search image of the food item they want, based on certain key elements of the natural food: its size, shape, and how it moves or doesn't move, for example. Anything matching the search image triggers the fish to eat it. When trout are selective and hard to catch, a successful fly must match the search image they have formed of the natural insect they are eating. In addition, the fly must be presented with the movement that matches that of the search image.

Based on my own experience and that of other accomplished fly fishers, the key characteristics of a natural that a fly should match when fish are feeding selectively are, in order of importance, its size, shape or silhouette, movement or action, and color. I find it interesting that most fly fishers spend a lot of time trying to

*An abundance of a single species of insect, in this case net-spinning caddisfly larvae (*Hydropsyche sp.*), triggers selective feeding by trout, which means your fly needs to match it to be successful.*

**Key Features of
Successful Fly Patterns**
(in order of importance)

1. Size
2. Shape
3. Movement
4. Color

match the color of the pattern to the natural, but then use a fly that is one or two sizes bigger or smaller or has a much different shape in the water. Though color is worth paying attention to, it is often the least important feature of a successful fly pattern. And don't forget your presentation. Where and how your fly moves in the water is usually critical to your success.

Do fish feed selectively on nymphs like they do on emergers or adults? I believe the answer is a definite yes. Here again, it occurs when a certain nymph is so abundant that fish save energy by feeding on it selectively. Therefore, it pays to know what nymphs are most abundant in the stream you are fishing. This requires spending some time collecting insects. It takes only twenty or thirty minutes to assess how rich a stream is in food and what nymphs or larvae are most abundant. With this information, your chances of selecting an effective pattern increase dramatically.

CHAPTER THREE

Tackle

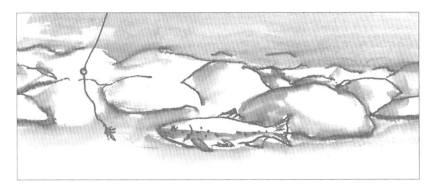

*Never forget that you, the fly-fisher, are the most important ingredient
of any tackle system, for you provide the knowledge, skill, and
energy to make the rest work. Other components are the rod, the
reel, the line and backing, and the leader and tippet.*

DAVE WHITLOCK, THE MASTERS ON THE NYMPH

We live in a world of specialization. Take tennis shoes. When I was a kid, I had one pair of tennis shoes that I used for baseball, basketball, football, riding my bike, running around the block, going fishing, and yes, playing tennis. Now jump ahead forty years. Today I own a different specialized pair of shoes for each activity. The gear of every activity I can think of, including fly fishing, has followed a similar route of specialization. When I first started fly-fishing about forty years ago, the idea of using different rods for different types of fishing didn't exist. You bought one all-around rod for where you lived. For me, growing up in Illinois farm country, that meant an 8-foot fiberglass rod that I used to deliver small nymphs and little poppers to bluegills, large streamers and big poppers to largemouth bass, and weighted jigs to crappie and white bass. It never occurred to me that I could use, let alone need, different rods for different types of fishing.

Now don't get me wrong. I'm not saying that the specialized equipment we have today, whether it's shoes or rods, hasn't improved performance. There's no question that it has. But it's also a common belief today that you must have the right specialized shoe or rod before you can even begin a certain activity, and this simply isn't true. So as you read about tackle for nymph fishing, keep in mind that you can successfully fish nymphs with just about any type of balanced fly-rod outfit, though some will allow you to do so more effectively and with less effort.

My favorite outfit for nymph fishing consists of a 9-foot, 6-weight, medium-action graphite rod; 6-weight, weight-forward floating line; 10- to 12-foot tapered leader with a 3X to 5X tippet; small (1/4 to 1/2 inch) red corkie strike indicator; and small split shot added eight to ten inches from the fly as needed for weight. Not only is this a great outfit for nymph fishing, but without the strike indicator and split shot, it will handle most any dry-fly or wet-fly situation for trout, take summer steelhead, and even throw streamers and poppers for bluegills and bass. Though I use this outfit for perhaps 75 percent of my nymph fishing and wouldn't feel handicapped very often if it were the only outfit I had, it isn't the only one I use. Depending on the type of stream I'm fishing or technique I'm using, my rod might range from a 4- to an 8-weight and from 7 1/2 to 9 1/2 feet long, with a double-taper or a weight-forward floating, sinking-tip or full-sinking line. To help decipher what makes a good nymph-fishing outfit, let's look at each part individually.

The Rod

The rod, more than any other part of your outfit, determines how well you can fish different flies in different types of water. For nymph fishing, the first characteristic

I look for is a slow to medium rather than a fast action. This is partly personal preference. I grew up fly-fishing when slow fiberglass rods were the norm, and my casting stroke, for better or worse, evolved to match this slower pace. Nevertheless, for nymph fishing, a slow rod provides some distinct advantages over a fast one. First, a slow rod produces a wider loop in your line while casting. Most of us were instructed to cast a nice, tight loop. This is fine when fishing dry flies and you need to dry the fly with a few quick false casts before making a delicate accurate presentation. For nymph fishing, however, you want to minimize false casting, so there is no need for quick false casts between presentations. Plus, when you have a strike indicator and split shot on your leader, a tight loop often becomes a tangled mess. A wide loop significantly reduces the chance of indicator, fly, and split shot wrapping together. Such tangles often cause anglers to give up nymph fishing before they ever really get started. Second, a slow rod results in fewer broken tippets on the strike. This is especially helpful when a big fish grabs your fly and you are anticipating a much smaller one. Something has to give, and if it's not the rod, it will probably be the tippet. Finally, a slower rod takes less effort to cast when you are using heavy flies and extra weight on the leader.

The next consideration is rod length. A long rod helps you mend your line, control your drift, and set the hook. When I'm fishing medium to large rivers with few overhanging trees, I prefer a 9-foot rod. Longer rods also work well, but they often feel too heavy for my tastes. When fishing small streams with lots of trees and vegetation on the banks, a shorter rod, 7 to 8 feet, will help you stay out of the leaves.

Finally, you need to choose a rod for a particular line weight. Heavier lines cast heavier flies more effectively and with less effort. Given that most of the time when fishing nymphs, you will be casting weighted flies with split shot added to the leader, a 2- or 3-weight rod is not going to be your go-to nymph rod. To me, a 6-weight rod-and-line combination provides maximum flexibility in the range of flies it will easily cast. When fishing in a big river with large flies and a lot of weight added to sink them, a 7- or 8-weight rod and line will work better. Conversely, if you fish small streams with small nymphs, a 4- or 5-weight rod and line will perform well. My second most frequently used rod for nymphing is an 8½-foot-long 4-weight. Though I

A long rod, 8½ to 9½ feet, provides more control when fishing large rivers.

On small streams, a short rod of 7 to 8 feet will help you stay out of the trees and branches.

enjoy fishing this rod with nymphs in the right conditions, it is not nearly as versatile as my 9-foot 6-weight.

With the hundreds of quality rods available today, you will find many that work well for nymph fishing. The trick is to find one that you feel really comfortable with. This is no easy task. If you are a beginning fly fisher, the most versatile option would probably be a medium-action, 9-foot,

Today's market offers numerous kinds of rods. Cast a variety of different sizes and brands before making your final selection.

6-weight rod. If you have been fly-fishing for a while and want something specifically for nymph fishing, consider a slow-action rod in a length and line weight best suited for the types of streams and flies you fish most often. Whether you are new to fly fishing or an old-timer, it is always helpful to cast and fish with different rods so you can determine what fits your own casting style and needs the best. Go to fly shops and try out different types of rods. When fishing with friends, ask if they will let you try their rods for a few casts. If it happens to be a brand new rod, however, don't be surprised if your friend looks at you as if you were an in-law asking if it's okay to move in with him.

The Line

The weight of the rod you choose determines the weight of the line you need to use. Your next line decision is whether to get a floating or sinking line. If you need a single basic outfit, buy a floating line. I use a floating line 95 percent of the time for nymph fishing in streams or rivers. The rest of the time varies among a sinking-tip, full-sinking, and lead-core shooting taper, depending on how big and fast the river is and how deep I have to get my fly. But

There are dozens of lines the nymph fisher can choose from. For most applications, pick a floating line that matches the weight of the rod you'll be using.

deciding whether or not to use a sinking line depends on more than just how deep you need to fish. Though you can sink your fly quicker and deeper with a sinking line, you give up considerable line control and sensitivity in detecting strikes. Therefore, when fishing streams and rivers, I prefer a floating line until conditions demand switching to a sinking line. Lake fishing, however, is different. Fish in lakes routinely hold at a certain depth zone, so the most effective line is the one that gets to that depth quickly and stays there. This means you will need a variety of sinking lines.

After deciding on a floating or sinking line, you need to choose a line taper, most of which fall into one of two categories: double-taper or weight-forward. Double-taper lines have the same gradual taper at both ends and an even running line section in the middle. They mend easily and allow delicate presentations. Weight-forward lines have a quick taper at the front end, followed by a gradual taper to a long section of even running line, which puts most of the weight closer to the front. As a result, weight-forward lines handle wind and heavier flies better than double-tapers. Since a delicate presentation is rarely a concern when nymph fishing, I usually use weight-forward lines. On spring creeks and small streams, I often use a lighter rod to cast small nymphs to trout I have spotted, which requires the same kind of delicate presentations as dry-fly fishing, and here a double-taper line usually works best. A weight-forward line will likely be your first choice for most nymph fishing, but as with rods, experiment with different line tapers as well.

The Leader

In fly fishing, leaders do more than just connect your fly to the line. To create a balanced, efficient casting outfit, the rod, line, and leader all must work together, and the leader forms the last important link to your fly. A properly designed leader allows the flow of energy from the line to reach your fly, causing it to land gently on the water at the end of a fully extended leader and not in a tangled pile.

There are two basic types of leaders: tapered and straight. Tapered leaders cast easier and are your best choice for most nymph-fishing techniques. The tapered leader has a large-diameter butt section attached to the fly line, then gradually tapers down to a uniform small-diameter section 3 to 6 feet long, the tippet. The tippet size should be selected based on the size and weight of fly you are casting: Large or heavy flies require large-diameter tippets, and small, lightweight flies require small-diameter tippets. Tippet sizes range from 8X to 0X; the larger the number, the smaller the diameter of the tippet. The accompanying table is a general guide to tippet sizes for various hooks. The hook sizes listed for each tippet diameter are general suggestions. The actual breaking strength, or test, of each tippet size varies among manufacturers and therefore is not listed.

A wide selection of leaders is available to fly fishers. In most cases, a 9- to 10-foot tapered leader works well for nymph fishing.

Tippet size	Diameter (in inches)	Use for hook sizes
8X	.003	24–26–28
7X	.004	20–22–24
6X	.005	16–18–20
5X	.006	14–16–18
4X	.007	10–12–14
3X	.008	8–10–12
2X	.009	6–8–10
1X	.010	4–6–8
0X	.011	2–4–6

Other considerations when selecting tippet size include wind and leader shyness of the fish. A slightly heavier tippet is needed to cast well into a strong wind. How easily fish see the leader is usually more of an issue when fishing dry flies than with nymphs, though I have run into situations in clear spring creeks where dropping down to a smaller-diameter tippet improved my nymph fishing. In most situations, fish seem less put off by a leader underwater than by one lying on the surface, but not always.

Fluorocarbon leaders have been available for a number of years and have gained some strong proponents. Like any new technology, they have pluses and minuses. The big plus is how transparent and invisible they are underwater, the main reason for using them. When fish are extremely leader-shy, a fluorocarbon leader can be a big help. On the minus side, fluorocarbon is more brittle and lacks the stretch of monofilament and thus is less forgiving when striking or playing a fish. This is another case where a slow-action rod is a benefit. Knots must be tied more carefully with fluorocarbon to avoid unexpected separation of your fly from your tippet. Another drawback is expense. If you are nymph-fishing in moderate to fast water, you will gain little advantage from using a fluorocarbon leader. If, however, you are casting in vain to selective trout in a clear, slow-moving stream or lake and have already dropped down to the finest monofilament tippet you can practically use, switching to a fluorocarbon leader might just save the day.

Tapered leaders come in two styles: knotless or knotted. Knotless leaders are machine-made from a single continuous strand of monofilament that tapers from the butt to the tippet. Knotted leaders are constructed from individual segments of different-size leader material, knotted together from a thick butt section to a fine tippet. The lengths of individual segments vary depending on the overall length of the leader. Both knotless and knotted leaders can be purchased ready to fish in many lengths and sizes. One advantage of knotted leaders is that you can construct them yourself to any length and taper design you want. Knotted leaders also turn over heavy flies somewhat better than knotless, but knotless leaders provide more delicate presentations. Either works well for most nymph-fishing situations.

Straight leaders are made from a single strand of even-size leader material cut to whatever length you need. Though rarely used for dry-fly or wet-fly fishing because of their poor ability to turn over the fly on long casts, they are preferred for some nymph-fishing methods, such as the Czech nymphing technique. The main advantage is that a straight leader sinks faster than a tapered leader, a valuable benefit when you need to get a nymph to the bottom quickly.

You must decide what length of leader to use. Most of the time, I use a 9- to 12-foot leader when I'm nymph-fishing with a floating line on medium to large rivers. On occasions where I need to be more careful not to spook fish, such as when fishing spring creeks with small nymphs near the surface, I might use a leader 12 to 14 feet long. Longer leaders are rarely needed for stream fishing, but for lake fishing I have used leaders up to 30 feet long to get my nymphs to the desired depth. When I'm fishing small streams, I shorten the leader to just 6 to 8 feet long. With sinking-tip or full-sinking lines, you need to use a really short leader only 3 or 4 feet long so that the fly does not float up above the depth of the sinking line.

Whenever you are experiencing casting problems or difficulty controlling the drift of your fly, take a close look at your leader. In many cases, making your leader longer or shorter or changing the tippet diameter or length will solve the problem.

Strike Indicators

It is more than likely that at some point in your nymph fishing, you will use a strike indicator. It is interesting how much angst such a small device stirs up in some fly fishers. A few anglers who have accepted nymph fishing as a legitimate fly-fishing method still can't accept the use of a strike indicator. If using one is unethical and immoral, I plead guilty, for over the years a strike indicator has become a standard part of my nymph-fishing equipment. Once I started using a strike indicator, after nymph-fishing for years without one, my success improved dramatically, and I realized just how many fish I had been missing. The problem became even clearer to me when I put on a wet suit, mask, and snorkel and watched fish react to an angler's nymph underwater. A highly experienced angler was fishing a large nymph in a stream abundant with trout. From my vantage point underwater, I was able to watch trout after trout completely inhale the large nymph and instantly spit it back out without the slightest hint of detection on the part of the angler. It was only when there was no slack in his line and leader that he was able to detect the trout's advances.

An indicator adjusted to the proper distance from the fly eliminates slack in the leader and thus greatly improves your chances of detecting unnatural movement of your fly. My underwater observations clearly showed that any slack in the leader prevented the angler from detecting a strike at least 80 percent of the time. In other words, eight out of ten fish that grab your nymph go completely undetected. This explains why, when nymphing, most anglers hook fish after the fly has drifted downstream and starts to swing to the surface. The rising action of the fly may be part of the reason so many fish are hooked at this point in the drift, but I believe another key reason is that the slack is finally out of the leader and you can actually detect the strike. Using an indicator greatly improves your chances of detecting strikes on the upper half of the fly's drift as well. If you feel, however, that an indicator gives you an unfair advantage or in some way violates your sense of fly-fishing ethics, you can still catch fish without using one; just don't be surprised if you catch less than those of us who do.

A wide variety of strike indicators are readily available in any fly-fishing shop. The best choice is partly determined by the particular nymphing technique you are using, but mostly it is personal preference. The larger or bulkier the indicator, the better it may float but the more difficult it will be to cast. This is the problem I have with most yarn indicators. Though they float well, they have more wind resistance and thus cast less efficiently. I prefer a small corkie or twist-on indicator. The advantage of the twist-on style is that you can add or remove it from your leader without removing your fly. More times than I care to admit, in my excitement to start fishing, I have tied on my flies and added split shot, only to realize that I forgot to put on my corkie indicator. When that happens, I grab a twist-on indicator and pretend that's what I

Several different kinds of indicators are available. Clockwise from top left: *white yarn; Biostrike indicator putty; red yarn; black and white yarn; red twist-on; rubber indicators in three colors; various sizes and colors of corkies.*

An indicator made from foam tubing floats well and is sensitive, but you should rig this up before you go fishing.

intended to use all along. If they are not correctly twisted onto your leader, however, twist-ons have a habit of flying off during the cast.

An indicator that will never fly off is a piece of foam tubing, 1 to 1 1/2 inches long, threaded onto your leader with a needle. Friction from the foam against the leader keeps it in place, but you can still slide it easily up or down the leader when needed. Because this takes more time to set up, I like to prepare leaders with foam-tube indicators ahead of time and keep them in a pocket of my vest ready to use. The only way to determine what indicator works best for you is to experiment with all the various types. This may sound like work, but remember, you'll be fishing during the whole experiment.

Once you've settled on the type of indicator, you also need to choose a size and color. I prefer small indicators. They cast better, make less disturbance landing on the water, and still float well with all but really large and heavy nymphs. By small, I mean about 3/8 inch in diameter for corkies and about 1/2 inch long for twist-ons. For foam-tube indicators, I use 1/4 -inch-diameter tubing about 1 1/2 inches long. I've tried different colors over the years and seem to keep coming back to basic red, which shows up best in a wide variety of water and lighting conditions. There are no right or wrong choices, so experiment with different sizes and colors.

How far up the leader should you put your indicator? My general rule of thumb is to place it approximately twice the distance from the fly as the depth of the water I am fishing. In other words, if you are fishing in water three feet deep, place the indicator six feet from your fly. This distance needs to be adjusted slightly as you move to slower or faster water. In slower water, the indicator should be closer to the fly; in faster water, place it farther away. The goal is to provide enough distance so that the fly reaches the bottom with no slack in the leader between the indicator and fly. One way to tell if you have the dis-

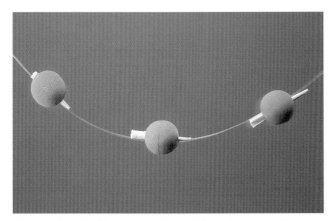

Two or three indicators can be used in calm water for even greater strike sensitivity.

tance right is to set it farther away than you think is needed and allow your fly to gently snag the bottom. Then shorten the distance and see if the fly still snags the bottom. When it just ticks the bottom occasionally without getting caught on it, you have just the right distance between your fly and indicator for that depth and current speed. With practice, this becomes a relatively quick process.

What about using more than one indicator? This may sound like too much of a good thing, especially if you already have reservations about using one strike indicator. Nevertheless, I have met several superb nymph fishermen over the years that used two, and sometimes three, small corkie indicators placed about three inches apart. The idea behind this approach is that you watch for a change in position between the indicators during their drift. Since most fish strikes cause only the slightest movement to your indicator, it can be difficult to see if it has moved a little to the right or left or slowed down or sped up. But if you have two or three indicators near each other, you can more easily see if one moves slightly relative to another. After using this method myself, I can say that it does work. I find it works best, however, in areas with moderate to slow current and a smooth surface. In fast and somewhat turbulent water, the indicators bounce around too much for their movement relative to each other to be meaningful.

Weight

There is only one reason for adding weight to your fly or leader: to get your fly deeper, quicker. Often this is the single most important ingredient to successful nymph fishing. It wouldn't make sense to fish an unweighted nymph six inches below the surface when fish are feeding two feet deep. You wouldn't catch many fish with this approach. The same problem occurs when fish are feeding near the bottom in three feet of water and your fly,

weighted though it may be, sinks only one or two feet deep. Even if your nymph perfectly matches what the trout are taking, you will catch few to no fish if your fly drifts one or two feet above their heads.

There are only two places to add weight: to your fly and to your leader. I tie most of my nymphs with some added weight. This may be in the form of lead wire wrapped around the shank, beadheads (tungsten beads are particularly heavy), lead-ball eyes, or cones. I also try to keep the fly's proper silhouette, so I don't wrap lead wire around the shank of a nymph that should have a slender body shape. I keep some nymphs unweighted so I can fish effectively near the surface when needed.

Most of the time, the problem is too little weight rather than too much. Unless you are using really large, heavily weighted flies, you will probably need to add weight to the leader in addition to using a weighted nymph. The added weight may make casting more difficult and less enjoyable, but catching fish is more enjoyable than just casting. If you want to catch fish with nymphs, you must get your fly to their level.

Weight for leaders comes in a variety of forms, including split shot, lead strips, and lead putty. All of these add weight effectively, so the choice is again mostly one of personal preference. Whatever you select, use weight made of tin or other lead-substitute material, as enough lead can be lost in streams to pollute the water. My preference is small tin split shot in sizes from BB (0.4 gram) to 4 (0.2 gram). The key is to add enough weight to sink your fly to the proper depth. The amount of weight needed depends on the weight of the fly, the depth you are trying to reach, and the current speed; the faster the water, the more

Keep your split shot close enough to your fly that your fly reaches the same depth as your lead weight. Six to ten inches is about right.

weight you'll need. The particular technique you are using also influences how quickly and how deep your nymph will sink, but for the most part, it is how much everything weighs that determines the depth your fly will reach. A basic rule of thumb I use is that if my fly is not touching or snagging the bottom every four or five casts, I need to add more weight to fish near the bottom effectively.

A frequent question about adding weight to the leader is how far from the fly to put the weight. I prefer to place it relatively close to the fly—six to ten inches up the leader. This keeps the fly at roughly the same depth underwater as the weight on the leader. When they get too far apart, the weight may be near the bottom, but your fly may be six to twelve inches higher and out of the proper depth.

A simple split shot or lead strip may seem like a very minor part of your overall nymph-fishing gear, but the amount of weight you use has a major impact on your success. You should always keep aware of it and adjust the weight depending on the weight of your fly, the type of water you are fishing, and how deep the fish are feeding.

Knots

Attaching all the parts of a fly-fishing outfit together requires knots. Knots aren't so important in catching fish, but they sure are important when it comes to landing them. How often have you lost a good fish because your fly or leader broke off at a knot? The knot you use can also affect the action of your fly underwater and therefore how natural it looks to the fish. There are dozens of knots you can use, and I haven't tested all the different kinds for their strength as some anglers have, so I will say only a few things about them.

For attaching my fly to the tippet, especially for nymph fishing, I prefer a knot that leaves a small loop at the eye of the fly rather than one that is tight against the eye, as the loop allows greater movement of the fly under-

The Duncan loop is one knot that allows the fly to move freely as it drifts, providing more lifelike action.

water. I have used a Duncan loop knot for years and find it quite satisfactory, though recent articles on the topic suggest the nonslip mono loop knot is stronger. For tying tippet and leader segments together, I prefer a uni-knot and find it superior to the frequently used blood knot or double surgeon's knot. Knot tests I have seen recently suggest, however, that the uni-knot is less than ideal in terms of breaking strength and recommend the ligature knot. As there is always room for improvement, I will try these new knots and change if they work better and I can get my feeble mind to learn how to tie them.

No matter which knots you use, spend some time at home tying them until they become second nature. If you have frequent break-offs while playing fish, it's time to pay closer attention to your knots. It's usually not your knot's fault for not staying knotted. There are many excellent books on knots and plenty of information on websites that show how to tie them.

CHAPTER FOUR

Selecting the Right Pattern

There is absolutely nothing so intoxicating to the fly-fisherman as
to have firm proof that his fly works and also to know what it was
that the fish took it for. From that day forward I was and am a firm
believer in trying to match the prevalent nymph in a given piece
of water and I soon found that the more I succeeded in that,
the fewer fishless days I encountered.

CHARLES E. BROOKS, *NYMPH FISHING FOR LARGER TROUT*

Most fly fishers begin nymph fishing with the idea that trout aren't picky about what they eat underwater. In fact, most of us have a hard time convincing ourselves that any trout worthy of its genes would ever turn down a large, juicy-looking morsel drifting by its nose, regardless of how different that juicy morsel might look from what it has been eating. After all, food is food, beggars can't be choosers, and all that, right? What we tend to forget is that in most healthy trout streams, food is plentiful and trout don't have to grab the first thing that drifts by. Nymphs, like adults during a hatch, peak in abundance and availability at different times of the day and different times of the year, and when one particular type of nymph is available, it is more efficient for a trout to become selective, focusing its attention on just that one type of food and ignoring everything else, even that large, juicy morsel you tossed at him.

If choosing an effective nymph pattern depends on knowing something about the insects in the stretch of stream you are fishing, what do you need to know and how do you get the information? As when selecting any kind of fly pattern, you need to answer just two questions: What insects are most abundant, and of those abundant, which ones are most available? The first question is easier to answer, so let's start there.

To get a good idea of what nymphs are most common or abundant in the stream you are fishing, you need to put your rod down and spend some time collecting bugs. I know this may be hard to do. After all, we never get to fish as much as we would like to, so once we get to a stream, we don't really want to put aside fishing for something like bug collecting. But if you want to include catching in your definition of fishing, you will find the time well spent.

I have found one approach that seems to help. Don't worry about collecting bugs right away. Go ahead and fish for an hour or so, keeping track of the number of fish you catch. If you catch a lot of fish, then you have it right, and collecting bugs really isn't necessary. If, however, you catch no fish or only one or two, then put down your rod and spend the next half hour collecting bugs to see what fly pattern you should be using and how you should be fishing it. With this information in hand, put on a new pattern and start fishing again. After another hour or so, you'll know if collecting has helped you catch more fish. There are no sure things in fishing, but getting the information you need to select an appropriate nymph pattern won't take more than twenty or thirty minutes of your time, and it can easily improve your fishing success.

Collecting Specimens

There are several things to consider before collecting a few samples of insects from a stream. First, make sure it is legal. Some states have laws that require anyone collecting aquatic organisms, including insects, from any body of water to get a collecting permit. These laws are usually in place to regulate commercial collecting of certain species for bait, prevent the introduction of species from one region to another where they are not native, or avoid disturbing habitat when and where sensitive fish species are spawning. Though I have never heard of a fisherman getting pinched for picking up some rocks to look at what's crawling on them, you might want to check existing state game laws to learn what's allowed and what isn't.

Once you've made sure you won't go to jail for collecting a few bugs, you need to find a good location where you can get a representative sample of whatever lives in the stream. The best habitat to collect from is usually moderately fast riffles, six inches to two feet deep, with a gravel to cobble bottom. Such riffles generally produce the majority of insects drifting in the current and will thus provide a good sample of the nymphs available for trout to eat. Shallow, moderately fast riffles are also easy to wade and sample, whereas collecting nymphs from the bottom of a deep pool can present a few problems.

Once you have picked a riffle to sample, select four to six different locations in the riffle to collect samples. Choose a couple sites close to shore in relatively slow, shallow water. Near-shore areas often harbor mature nymphs that have migrated close to the bank in preparation for emergence. Spread the other samples around the riffle so that you sample a range of depths, velocities, and sizes or types of substrate. Your goal is to get a good idea of the diversity of nymphs living in the riffle and which ones are most numerous. Looking at samples from a variety of locations will give you the best understanding of what trout are most likely seeing and eating.

Riffles from a few inches to about knee-deep are generally good places to stop and view the bugs. CAROL HORVATH

Though most trout streams have a mixture of riffle, run, and pool habitats, some, such as low-gradient meadow streams and gently flowing spring creeks, completely lack riffles. In such streams, collect samples from a variety of different substrate types. Wood, aquatic plants, roots and debris around undercut banks, decaying leaves and organic matter all provide good homes for nymphs that end up as food for trout. The habitat you sample will vary depending on what is present in different streams; just try to collect from a cross section of whatever is available.

Technique and Equipment

The technique you use to collect samples depends on how involved and how accurate you want to be. As you might guess, the more accurate you want to be, the more involved the collecting technique becomes. The most involved approach is still easy to do; you just need to take along a bit more equipment. The simplest method involves wading out to different areas in a riffle, picking up a few loose rocks from the bottom, and quickly scanning them for whatever nymphs are clinging to their sides. This approach requires no extra equipment and takes little time, but it provides minimal information. The nymphs most available to trout are the most active ones, and they often let go of the rock before you even get it out of the water. Therefore, you get a limited and often mistaken view of what nymphs are present.

A much more effective approach is to hold some kind of net next to the stream bottom, perpendicular to the current, while you or a friend disturbs the substrate upstream of the net. The current washes all the dislodged insects into the net, which you then carefully lift out of the water and observe what nymphs are present. A variety of different types of nets can be used:

- Small, collapsible kick nets. Most fly shops sell small, foldable kick nets that easily fit in a vest. I have found the majority of these adequate for catching nymphs, pupae, or adults drifting near the surface but too small to be of much use for collecting nymphs from the bottom of a stream. If you want a net for bottom sampling, I recommend using one about two feet high by eighteen inches to two feet wide.
- Noncollapsible kick nets. A more substantial kick net can easily be made at home from a three-foot square of fiberglass window screen attached to two four-foot-long, one-inch-diameter wooden dowels. These nets collect stream samples very effectively but are a little bulky to carry around while you are fishing.
- D-frame aquatic net. This is a commercially made net with a D-shaped metal hoop and a fine-meshed

net bag attached. They can be purchased from Wards Scientific Supply (www.wards.com) for about $40. Besides sampling riffles effectively, they can be used to sample slow water, including lakes, by swishing the net through debris and aquatic plants. This may be the most versatile net, but it is too large to slip into a vest.

This collapsible kick net takes a good sample and will fold up small enough to fit into a fishing vest. CAROL HORVATH

A homemade kick net works great but is a bit too big to easily carry while fishing. CAROL HORVATH

A D-frame kick net for collecting and white tray for viewing make a great combination.

I usually carry a collapsible kick net in my vest when I'm walking along a stream. When I'm close to a car or fishing out of a boat, I keep a D-frame net handy as well. A few other items besides a collecting net are also useful and can easily fit in your vest:

- Tweezers. Tweezers always come in handy for picking up small nymphs for a closer look or transferring the insects from net to vial for later study.
- Small, white tray or dish. Even in a net, nymphs are not easy to see. If you place the live nymphs in a white dish with about $1/2$ inch of water, you will be able to see them clearly and get a more accurate view of their size, color, and behavior. You can also drop your fly patterns into the dish right next to the naturals and see how close your flies look to the real thing.
- Small magnifying glass. A 10X or 15X magnifying glass or jeweler's loupe (I prefer a 10X loupe) will provide you a closer, and often fascinating, view of the nymphs in the tray.

Once you have a net full of insects, a pair of tweezers will make catching some for closer examination much less frustrating.

Viewing nymphs in a white tray or jar lid with some water allows you to observe details you can't see if they are left in a net.

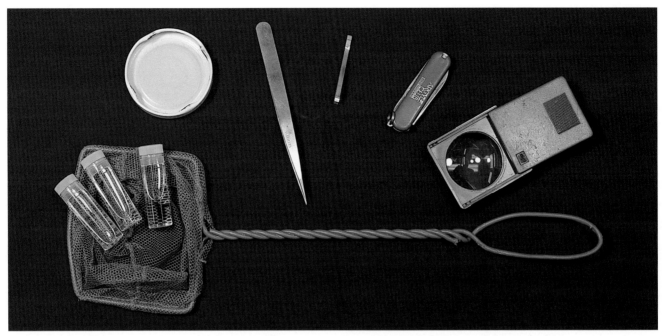

These items easily fit in a vest and come in handy for observing and collecting specimens. DAVE HUGHES

Though collecting a few kick samples from a productive riffle will have no harmful effects on the stream's aquatic life, use some caution and common sense. Avoid taking samples where and when trout or other fish may have recently spawned. Collecting kick samples could easily damage eggs buried in the gravel. Do not disturb sensitive plant communities growing on the stream bottom when you take your samples. These plant communities may take weeks or more to recover from rough treatment. If a lot of anglers kick and disturb them, they may never recover. After you have finished observing the insects you collected, return them to the stream unharmed. Releasing the insects back into the stream is just as important to your fishing as releasing the fish you catch.

Preserving Aquatic Insects

Keeping a few specimens for a collection and further study will not negatively impact a stream's bug population. It is a simple activity many anglers find fascinating and useful. Well-cared-for samples can be helpful when you get back home for tying fly patterns, and you can identify them to learn more about what is living in your streams. If you start keeping a collection, it's important to follow the simple guidelines below. If you do, your collection will grow in value and usefulness over the years. If you don't, you will end up with a box full of dried-up specimens that you will toss in the garbage.

- If you collected butterflies as a kid, you will remember drying and pinning the specimens for display. Unlike terrestrial insects, aquatic insects—nymphs,

larvae, pupae, and adults—must be kept in a liquid preservative rather than pinned and dried. The bodies of aquatic insects are too soft and simply shrivel up when dried.

- The best all-around preservative for aquatic insects is 80 percent ethyl alcohol. Denatured ethanol, treated with additives so it cannot be consumed, is available at most drug stores. A simple alternative is isopropyl, or rubbing alcohol, but it dries out specimens more than ethanol, causing delicate legs and tails of specimens to break off more easily. Other solutions are occasionally recommended for storing aquatic insects because they do not fade or change the colors of specimens like alcohol. The problem is that these solutions often use formaldehyde and other rather toxic chemicals, and they still change colors to some degree. In the end, 80 percent ethyl alcohol is the best and safest preservative I have found.

- Small glass vials with leakproof lids are best for storing specimens. I prefer one-dram shell vials with plastic snap-on lids. Most vials with screw-on caps do not seal tightly enough, and the preservative evaporates from the vial in a few weeks or months, reducing the specimens inside into shriveled, dried-up clumps. For years I have used Kimble shell vials (stock #60965D-1) in the one-dram size. These are available from many scientific supply companies.

- All vials must be labeled correctly. This is a critical step if you plan to keep a collection. Small strips of twenty-five-pound white paper cut to fit inside the vials make good labels. Use a number-two lead pencil to record information on the labels before putting them inside the vials. Ink, even if it's alcohol-resistant, fades over time. On one side of each label, write the name of the lake or river, with river mile if known; county and state; date; and name of collector. On the other side, write the name of the specimen. Use the lowest level of identification you are certain of. For example, if all you know for sure is that it is a mayfly, then only put Ephemeroptera on the label. If you know it is one of the blue-winged olives but not sure which one, then put Ephemeroptera: Baetidae on the label. If you know for sure it is a western march brown, put *Rhithrogena morrisoni* on the label. Avoid using a common name unless it is the only name you know. Also include on the label the name of the person providing the identification. Here's an example of a properly completed label.

Side 1

> Rock Creek at RM 25, Walker County, OR
> November 18, 1985
> Collected by C. Horvath

Side 2

> *Drunella doddsi*
> Ephemeroptera: Ephemerellidae
> Determined by R. E. Hafele

Organizing Your Collection

It won't take long before you have dozens of vials with a wide variety of specimens collected from different locations at different times. To make your collection really worthwhile, you need some way to keep it organized so you know what you have and can easily find a particular specimen when you want. There are numerous ways you can organize a collection, and to a large degree the approach is a matter of personal preference. A simple method is to keep all the vials of a particular order, such as mayflies, stoneflies, or caddisflies, stored together.

This will only work to a point, however. Once you get a large number of vials of each order, you will have a hard time keeping track of them. It's a good idea, from the very beginning, to give each vial a unique number and keep a written record with information about what's in the vials in your collection, and where and when the specimens were collected. This can be kept in a bound notebook or on a computer spreadsheet. The advantage of the computer spreadsheet is that you can easily search your record of vials for a specific specimen or quickly create lists, such

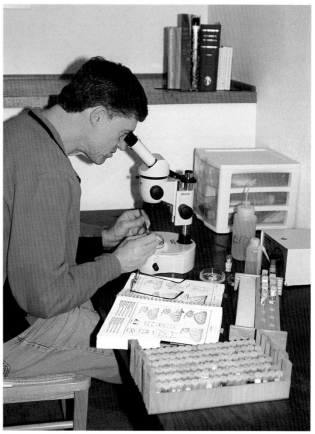

Checking insect identification with a microscope is a level of detail beyond what most anglers will ever go to. If you keep specimens for later study, however, label and store the vials so you can easily find what you collected. DAVE HUGHES

as all caddisflies collected in May. Add as much other information in your notebook or computer file as you wish. Notes about the weather, water temperature, fish activity, and effective fly patterns can expand your collection record into a valuable fishing log. An example of a record set up to organize a collection of specimens is shown on the following page.

Deciding Which Nymph to Imitate

Once you have taken samples from several different locations and placed specimens of the nymphs and pupae from each sample into a white tray with some water in roughly the same proportion as they occurred in the net, the question now becomes, what nymph out of the wide variety wiggling in the tray should you actually select to imitate? First you need to determine which bugs are most abundant and which are most available.

Deciding what's most abundant is simply a matter of visually evaluating the bugs in the tray and figuring out which one seems most numerous relative to the others. If you put the bugs into the tray in roughly the same pro-

Vial #	Specimen				Stage	Date collected	Location	Notes/ comments
	Order	Family	Genus/sp.	Common name				
1	Trichoptera	Rhyacophilidae	*Rhyacophila*	Green rock worm	Larva	5/16/99	Lost River, WA	Very warm day with no adult insect activity.
2	Diptera	Chironomidae	—	Midge	Pupa	2/23/01	Weber Lake, ID	Sunny & cold, fish rising 1–3 P.M. Had good success with black TDC pupa, size 18.

Keep a record of each specimen you collect. You can organize information like this in a notebook or computer spreadsheet.

portion as they occurred in the net, you will have a pretty accurate idea of what nymph is most abundant. Also keep in mind that size doesn't matter. In other words, don't give some bug extra credit because it's large compared with another one that's more numerous but much smaller. Focus your attention on which is most numerous.

Next, you need to decide which nymph, larva, or pupa is most available. The most abundant bug is not necessarily the most available. Though availability is partially determined by abundance, the primary factor is behavior. Some nymphs or larvae, for example, are active swimmers, while others burrow into the substrate. Basically, all nymphs or larvae can be classed into one of the following behavior types: swimmers, crawlers, clingers, or burrowers. Swimmers and crawlers, because of their more active lifestyle, will almost always be more available to trout than clingers or burrowers.

The maturity of nymphs or pupae also affects their availability. Mature nymphs or pupae can be recognized by how dark their wing pads look. Larvae have no wing pads, so you cannot use this characteristic until the pupal stage for insects that undergo complete metamorphosis. Very dark, almost black, well-formed wing pads indicate that a nymph or pupa is mature and nearly ready to emerge. At this stage of the life cycle, the activity level increases, and many species will begin moving underwater to more preferable habitat for emergence. This increase in activity significantly increases availability to fish. Therefore, always pay close attention to which nymphs or pupae in the tray of insects are mature and which ones aren't.

Another trait that influences availability is the feeding habits of different nymphs or larvae. Species that must move around to find their food will be more available than those that remain stationary for feeding. In general, predator species must move more than those that feed on plants or detritus, decaying organic material such as leaves and wood. For this reason, predaceous stoneflies such as golden stones (*Hesperoperla pacifica*

or *Calineuria californica*) will be available to fish more often than the detritus-eating salmonflies *(Pteronarcys californica)*. Feeding behavior isn't always an accurate indicator of availability, however. The net-spinning caddisflies (family Hydropsychidae), for example, feed by constructing small, spiderweblike nets on the sides of rocks in moderate to fast riffles. Food is strained from the water as it flows through the nets. This feeding mechanism doesn't require the caddis larvae to move, but forces them to stay put at their nets. The number of net-spinning caddis larvae often becomes so numerous on a single rock, however, that not all of them can find a suitable net-building site. As a result, the larvae must drift downstream to find a less crowded neighborhood. Such drift behavior increases their availability to trout. In fact, the propensity of a nymph or larva to drift may be the biggest factor affecting its availability.

Insect drift—behavioral drift, emergence drift, or surface drift—is the way to a trout's stomach, and species that drift more are much more available to feeding fish. Therefore, it is definitely helpful to know which insects drift and which don't. But drift is a complex behavior. Factors such as when drift occurs, how far individuals drift, and how they move in the drift all affect a nymph species' overall availability. Some interesting research has been done on this topic. One study evaluated the availability to trout of a wide range of aquatic insects found in Rocky Mountain trout streams. Based on a variety of factors, including drift propensity, drift distance, drift timing, size, mobility, emergence behavior, and ovipositing behavior, each insect's overall availability was assessed. The results are rather interesting. A total of ninety-five different aquatic insects were ranked. In the accompanying table, I have listed the fifty most available aquatic insects in their order of availability using information from this study. Some of those listed, such as the Empididae (dance flies) and Athericidae (snipe flies), are not well known to anglers, but for the most part, the insects with the greatest availability to trout are ones fly fishers routinely imitate.

Fifty Most Available Insects to Trout in a Rocky Mountain Trout Stream

Availability ranking	Most available taxa		Most available taxa cont.		Availability ranking
	Insect family or *genus*	Common name	Insect family or *genus*	Common name	
1	*Baetis*	Blue-winged olive	Lepidostomatidae	Little plain brown sedge	26
2	Simuliidae	Blackfly	*Limnephilus*	Weedy sedge	27
3	*Acentrella*	Blue-winged olive	Uenoidae	Autumn sedge	28
4	Chironomidae	Midge	Empididae	Dance fly	29
5	*Ephemerella*	Pale morning dun	Philopotamidae	Finger-net caddis	30
6	*Drunella*	Flavilinea & western green drake	Polycentropodidae	Little checkered summer sedge	31
7	Heptageniidae	March brown & pale evening dun	Orthocladiinae	Midge	32
8	*Paraleptophlebia*	Mahogany dun	Tanytarsini	Midge	33
9	*Ameletus*	Brown dun	Pteronarcyidae	Salmon fly	34
10	Amphipoda	Scuds	*Dicosmoecus*	October caddis	35
11	*Serratella*	Western dark Hendrickson	Psychodidae	Moth fly	36
12	*Sweltsa*	Little green stone	*Hesperophylax*	Silver stripe sedge	37
13	Athericidae	Snipe fly	Elmidae	Riffle beetle	38
14	Nemouridae	Little brown stone	Dryopidae	Long-toed water beetles	39
15	Perlodidae	Little yellow stone	*Diphetor*	Blue-winged olive	40
16	Brachycentridae	American Grannom	*Choroterpes*	Brown quill	41
17	Rhyacophilidae	Green rock worm	Isonychiidae	Great leadwing or slate drake	42
18	Hydropsychidae	Net-spinning caddis	*Attenella*	Small blue-winged olive	43
19	*Antocha*	Cranefly	Leptoceridae	Long-horn sedge	44
20	*Dicranota*	Cranefly	*Ecclisomyia*	Early western mottled sedge	45
21	*Limonia*	Cranefly	Muscidae	Common fly	46
22	*Pedicia*	Cranefly	Tanyderidae	Winter cranefly	47
23	Perlidae	Golden stonefly	*Petrophila*	Aquatic moth	48
24	Glossosomatidae	Saddle-case caddis	Deuterophlebiidae	Mountain midge	49
25	Helicopsychidae	Snail-case caddis	Psychomyiidae	Dinky purple-breasted sedge	50

Source: Rader, Russell B. "A functional classification of the drift: traits that influence invertebrate availability to salmonids," *Canadian Journal of Fisheries and Aquatic Sciences* 54 (1997): 1211–1234.

Seven of the ten most available insects listed are mayflies, which may partially explain why mayfly patterns play such an important role in fly fishing. Blackflies, midges, and scuds round out the top ten. The five most available insects are quite small—pale morning duns are the largest, and they reach only a size 16—which points out why small fly patterns are so often effective. Some of the least available invertebrates were snails, freshwater clams, and freshwater worms. These all occur in slow water and often burrow into the substrate, traits that provide little opportunity for trout to find and feed on them.

Some common insects imitated by fly fishers were not ranked in this study because they did not occur in the streams being studied. Burrowing mayflies, for example, were not present and therefore not ranked. Because the nymphs burrow, they are not available to trout until emergence, when the nymphs leave the stream or lake bottom and swim up to the surface. Though this list is limited to Rocky Mountain trout streams, many of the insects on it are widespread, so you can use this table to help determine which bugs in your tray rank high in availability in many North American trout streams.

Based on the insects you collected, you have determined what food source is most abundant, and based on their behavior and maturity, you have determined what's most available. Now it's time to choose patterns to match the most abundant and most available nymphs. To help clarify this process a little further, below are analyses of actual insect samples collected from two different streams, along with my recommendations of which fly patterns to choose to fish the streams where the samples were collected.

The results from these examples are typical in that two or three nymphs jump out as top candidates to imitate rather than a single insect. Since most healthy streams have a wide variety of species in them, it is rare to see just one nymph so dominant that it stands out as the only choice. By narrowing your choices down to two or three possible patterns, however, you greatly improve your chances of using an effective fly.

Where fishing regulations permit, you can increase your odds of imitating the most important nymph by using two, or even three, different flies. Two or three nymphs also sink to the bottom quicker than a single nymph and can sometimes attract more attention from fish. On the minus side, it is much easier to get tangled, sometimes hopelessly so, when casting multiple flies.

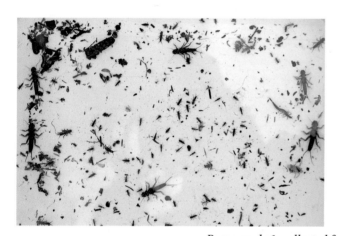 

Bug sample 1, collected from a large tailwater river.

Main Insects in Bug Sample 1

Common name	Genus/species	Abundance	Availability
Blue-winged olives	*Baetis tricaudatus*	High	High
Golden stones	*Hesperoperla pacifica*	High	Medium
Pale morning duns	*Ephemerella inermis*	Medium	High
Pale evening duns	*Heptagenia* sp.	Medium	Low
Brown duns	*Ameletus* sp.	Medium	Medium
Little yellow mays	*Epeorus* sp.	Low	Low
Green rock worms	*Rhyacophila* sp.	Low	High
October caddis	*Dicosmoecus* sp.	Low	Low

Based on abundance and availability, the three most important nymphs to imitate from this sample are blue-winged olives, golden stones, and pale morning duns. A size 18 Pheasant Tail, size 10 or 12 Brooks Golden Stone, and size 16 Beadhead Hare's Ear would be effective imitations for these nymphs, respectively.

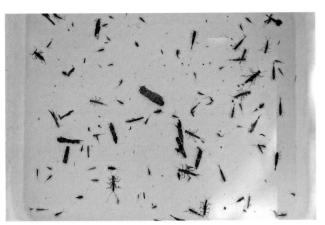

Bug sample 2, collected from a medium-size spring creek.

Main Insects in Bug Sample 2

Common name	Genus/species	Abundance	Availability
Blue-winged olives	*Baetis bicaudatus*	High	High
Brown duns	*Ameletus* sp.	High	Medium
Little yellow stones	*Skwala* sp.	High	Medium
Little yellow stones	*Yoroperla brevis*	Medium	Low
Lesser green drake	*Drunella coloradensis*	Low	Medium
Cased caddis	Limnephilidae	Medium	Low
Pale evening dun	*Heptagenia* sp.	Low	Low
October caddis	*Dicosmoecus* sp	Low	Low
Cased caddis	Leptoceridae	Low	Low

Based on the abundance and availability of insects in this sample, blue-winged olives would again be most important. This species of blue-winged olive is slightly larger than those in the first sample, and here a size 16 Pheasant Tail Nymph would be a good choice. Other important nymphs to imitate in this sample are the brown duns and little yellow stones. The brown duns could be imitated with a size 10 Muskrat or similar nymph. Little yellow stones are represented by two distinct types: *Skwala* and *Yoroperla*. *Skwala* is much more active and available than the *Yoroperla* and would be a better choice to imitate. A size 12 Yellow Stone Nymph would be appropriate.

One of the best examples of the benefits of using two nymphs occurred while I was fishing Rock Creek in Montana a few summers ago. Rock Creek is a productive trout stream with plenty of good riffle habitat. After spending twenty or thirty minutes checking out the bugs, I selected a couple patterns that matched the two most abundant and available nymphs. The water was two or three feet deep and fairly fast, so I needed a split shot above the first fly to sink the flies near the bottom. I was doing rather well catching nice, fat twelve- to fifteen-inch west-slope cutthroat wherever there was a good pocket of slower water along the bank or behind a boulder. Then I snagged something on the bottom and lost both flies. Since I had been catching nearly all the fish on just one of the two flies, I decided to save some time and rigged up with only that one fly. I added extra split shot so the fly would still sink to the bottom. Off I went fishing the same kind of water with the same fly pattern. Thirty minutes later—nothing. After a couple minutes thinking about what might be wrong, I decided to try an experiment. I rerigged with two flies, went back downstream a few hundred yards, and fished back up through the water I had just fished with a single nymph. To my surprise, on the third or fourth cast my indicator hesitated, and when I lifted up, a nice cutthroat bolted downstream. After three or four more fish, I went back to a single fly and again caught nothing. By adding more weight with the single fly, I felt certain I was getting to the same depth in both cases.

My conclusion was that somehow the trout found two flies drifting near each other more noticeable or enticing than a single fly drifting by itself. I can't prove my theory, but at the time it seemed the only logical explanation. I've certainly had other occasions where a single nymph worked just fine.

Trout Stream Insect Abundance

Determining the relative abundance of the insects you sampled will help you select an effective pattern. But the number and size of trout in a stream is a function of the amount of food present. Biologists report the abundance of aquatic invertebrates as the number of invertebrates per square meter of stream bottom or the weight, usually in grams, of invertebrates per square meter. The abundance of invertebrates varies widely among streams and different types of habitat in the same stream. In healthy trout streams, insect abundance may range from a few hundred individuals per square meter to more than five hundred thousand individuals per square meter. A variety of factors affect abundance, including temperature, nutrients, and sunlight, but one of the biggest factors is the substrate. An example of invertebrate abundance data collected from different stream substrates is given in the accompanying table. It shows that aquatic moss and plants have the highest densities of insects. This explains why spring creeks and tailwater streams, which often have aquatic plants, produce such prolific insect hatches. The lowest numbers of insects typically occur in sandy substrate.

Aquatic insect abundance also varies seasonally, and though actual abundance may vary widely among streams, most temperate trout streams show similar seasonal shifts in abundance. Changes in seasonal abundance are typically the result of common life cycle patterns among major groups of aquatic insects.

A study of seasonal abundance of insects in a few North Carolina trout streams showed a pattern typical of many freestone trout streams. Peak abundance occurred in the fall (September) and spring (April). High abundance in the fall was primarily due to increased numbers of caddisflies and two-winged flies (Diptera). Greater abundance in April was the result of increasing numbers of mayflies and two-winged flies. A significant drop in overall abundance occurred in May because of the spring emergence of numerous species. Numbers then gradually increased through the summer as eggs laid in the spring hatched. Following the peak in September, numbers again dropped, with the lowest of the year occurring during December and January. Abundance increased again in February and March, leading up to the peak in April.

Though this pattern in seasonal abundance may be common, it doesn't occur on all streams. Streams with unique temperature patterns generally show different cycles of seasonal abundance. Spring creeks and tailwater streams, which often have near-constant water temperatures or a shift from natural seasonal patterns, are good examples. Changes in seasonal temperature patterns cause shifts in insect life cycles and thus in seasonal abundance. Also, streams at higher elevations or latitudes than North Carolina may have a similar pattern, but it will be shifted slightly, with peaks in June and October instead of April and September. The common occurrence of fewer aquatic insects available for fish to feed on during the midsummer months happens to coincide with the peak period of abundance for terrestrial insects. A big part of the reason that terrestrial insects are important in the summer is that fewer aquatic insects are available for fish to eat.

How does the fluctuation in insect abundance affect your fishing? Primarily, it determines how finicky trout might be. Trout feeding becomes more selective when food is abundant. This means that the times of year when food is most abundant will also be when fish are most selective and your patterns and tactics will need to be more precise. It also explains why you might find trout unselective and seemingly easy to catch one day and a few weeks later very selective and difficult to catch.

Invertebrate	Number per square meter of stream bottom by substrate type			
	Cobblestones	Small gravel	Thick moss	Aquatic plants on stones
Mayflies	1,147	439	3,0236	15,858
Stoneflies	166	34	2,160	488
Caddisflies	895	877	2,5916	7,563
Diptera	663	202	183,574	105,395
Other (snails, worms, beetles, etc.)	232	1,822	190,054	114,666
Total	3,103	3,374	431,940	243,970

CHAPTER FIVE

Nymph-Fishing Tactics

In nature nothing happens without a reason. The difficulty for the angler is merely that the reason is hidden some way beneath the surface.

G.E.M. Skues, *The Way of a Trout with a Fly*

If you read various books and articles written about nymph fishing, you can easily find fifteen or twenty different nymph-fishing techniques described. So many, in fact, that you might feel dazed and confused about why and when different methods should be used. But all nymph-fishing techniques have the same simple goals: to select the right nymph pattern, usually one imitative of an abundant natural nymph; get the pattern to the depth and place where fish are feeding; fish the fly with a lifelike action; and be able to detect subtle strikes from unseen fish.

The only reason such a wide variety of techniques has evolved is that different methods are needed to accomplish these goals in different types of streams and different types of water. This chapter provides instructions on eleven different nymph-fishing techniques for various depths and water types. Some can be used across a relatively wide range of streams and water types; others are best suited to just a few.

Information about fish location, water type, and nymph-fishing tactics has been summarized in the accompanying table. Use the information to determine which technique is best suited to the type of water and depth of the fish where you are fishing. Once you know what technique to use for each water type, you will find nymph fishing not only effective, but also rather simple. Each method requires practice, however, in order to get consistent results. Having confidence that what you are doing will work is one of the keys to successful nymph

fishing. But confidence only comes from sticking with it long enough to prove to yourself it works by catching some fish. Therefore, don't give up after the first attempt or two without success. Study the methods, set yourself up with the right equipment, and give them a fair try. Believe me, they work.

Countdown Method

Some consider Ray Bergman to be the first person to describe the countdown method in his 1938 book *Trout*. Its effectiveness lies in the way it allows you to search out the depth at which fish are feeding, and then accurately return your fly to the same depth on repeated casts.

I have to admit, I rarely use this technique in streams and rivers, though I do use it when I'm fishing lakes. In streams, it is best suited for fishing near the bottom of deep pools in large rivers, something I tend to avoid since I find so many other habitats more productive and more interesting to fish in large rivers. If you need to fish a nymph or streamer near the bottom of a large, deep pool, however, this is an excellent technique to use.

EQUIPMENT NEEDED
Rod. A 6- to 8-weight, 8 to 9^1/$_2$ feet long, with enough backbone to cast a sinking line and medium to large weighted flies.
Line. When fishing water more than about 6 feet deep, a medium to fast full-sinking or sinking-tip, weight-

59

forward line works best. In pools or slow water less than 6 feet deep, you can usually get by with a floating line.

Leader. When using sinking-tip or full-sinking lines, a 3- to 4-foot leader is all that's needed. With a floating line, use a 10- to 14-foot leader. Use a tippet of 2X to 4X, depending on the size and weight of the fly being used.

Flies. Attractor flies and streamers often come into play when fishing large pools with this method. Woolly Bug-gers, Muddler Minnows, crayfish patterns, and Clouser Minnows are all flies that work well with this technique.

Approach

Position yourself slightly below and to the side of a large pool or eddy you intend to fish. Cast up and across the current, and as your line and fly begin sinking, start counting slowly to yourself. (You can count out loud, but

Nymph-Fishing Methods

Fish location (where you want your fly)	Water conditions		Hot spot type	Appropriate techniques
	Depth	Velocity		
Near the bottom	5–15 ft.	Slow	Pools in large to medium rivers	Countdown method
"	4–8 ft.	Medium–fast	Runs in large to medium rivers	Brooks method Shot and indicator
"	1–4 ft.	Medium–fast	Runs, riffles, and riffle tailouts	Shot and indicator Hinged leader Leisenring lift Hewitt method
"	2–6 ft.	Medium	Pocket water in runs or riffles	Shot and indicator High sticking Czech method
"	1–4 ft.	Slow–medium	Flats in large to medium rivers and pools in small streams	Hinged leader Sawyer method Leisenring lift Shot and indicator
Mid-depth, 2–3 feet deep	5–15 ft.	Slow	Pools	Hinged leader
"	2–4 ft.	Slow–medium	Flats	Sawyer method Hinged leader Leisenring lift
"	4–8 ft.	Medium–fast	Runs	Shot and indicator Hinged leader Leisenring lift
"	1–4 ft.	Medium–fast	Riffles and runs	Shot and indicator Hewitt method Leisenring lift
Near surface, in film to about 1 foot deep	5–10 ft.	Slow	Pools and flats	Wet-fly swing Skues method Leisenring lift
"	2–6 ft.	Medium	Flats and runs	Wet-fly swing Skues method Leisenring lift Hewitt method
"	1–4 ft.	Fast	Runs and riffles	Wet-fly swing Skues method Leisenring lift Hewitt method

your fishing partner may wonder whether you've been in the sun too long.) Depending how deep the water is and how much debris is on the bottom, begin by counting to ten and then increase the count by five on each successive cast until your fly touches the bottom or you find a depth with fish. An alternative approach is to keep counting on your first cast until you feel your fly touch bottom, then subtract two or three counts on your next cast. This will put your fly just off the bottom. Once you have established the proper count to get your fly to the desired depth, direct your casts in a fan shape around the pool to cover all the water.

To keep your fly at the desired depth during your retrieve, you need to adjust the speed based on the line you are using. A slow-sinking line requires a relatively slow retrieve to keep the fly near the bottom, and a fast-sinking line requires a faster retrieve. The size and weight of the fly also affect how fast you need to retrieve to maintain a consistent depth. If there is any current in the pool, the direction of your cast relative to the current is another fac-

The countdown method can be just the right approach for finding fish in a large, deep pool.

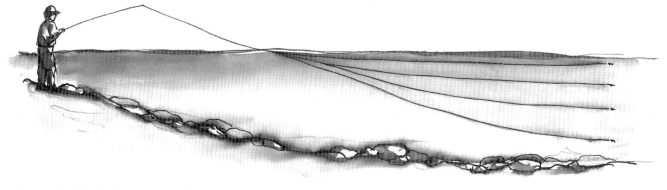

Change the depth of your retrieve by increasing or decreasing your count. Once you find a depth with fish, you can return your fly to the same depth by repeating the same count.

tor in how fast your line and fly sink. They will sink faster with a slightly upstream cast than one that is slightly downstream. Thus, to keep your fly at the same depth, you need to increase your count slightly as you move from casting up and across to down and across. Experiment with your count and retrieve speed for the best results.

Tips for Success

- Position yourself close to shore near the middle of a large pool or slow-water section of a river.
- Cast up and across, start counting slowly to ten or twenty, and then begin a slow to moderate retrieve. Increase the count if you wish to fish deeper, or decrease the count if you wish to fish shallower. In most cases, you want your fly close to the bottom. This requires sinking-tip or full-sinking lines in water more than about six feet deep.
- Make successive casts in a fan shape around the pool or river segment to completely cover the water.
- Try different fly patterns and types of retrieves—slow to fast and with or without twitches or jerks.

Shot and Indicator Method

This is the nymph-fishing technique I use most frequently in streams and rivers. The shot and indicator method can be used in slow- to fast-water habitats, in small to large streams and rivers, and for fishing near the bottom or closer to the surface. A common situation where this method is particularly useful is when you want to fish a nymph close to the bottom, one to four feet deep, in medium-fast runs, riffles, or riffle tailouts. The versatility and effectiveness of this method make it one you should definitely practice and become proficient at using.

I don't know who first developed this technique, but I do know it has been around in various forms for a long time. It often stirs the ire of dry-fly and even nymph-fishing purists who consider the use of an indicator an unnecessary or unethical aid. For better or for worse, I am not burdened by such feelings and consider this one of the most effective and exciting methods of taking trout.

EQUIPMENT NEEDED

Rod. A 4- to 8-weight, 8 to 9$^{1}/_{2}$ feet long, medium to slow action.

Line. A double-taper or weight-forward floating line.

Leader. Tapered leader 9 to 12 feet long for medium to large rivers, 6 to 8 feet long for small streams. Use a tippet of 2X to 6X, depending on the size and weight of the fly being used.

Indicator. Any style that best suits the water type and your personal preference, attached about twice the depth of the water away from your first fly.

Weight. Add shot or other weight to the leader 8 to 10 inches above the fly as needed to sink the fly to the appropriate depth.

Make an upstream mend to avoid current drag on the indicator.

Adjust the distance between your indicator and fly so there is little or no slack line in between but there is still enough leader to allow your fly to reach the bottom. One and a half to two times the depth of the water is usually about right. Strikes will typically be subtle, so watch your indicator for the slightest unnatural movement.

Flies. A wide range of sizes, styles, and colors can be used, usually selected to match the dominant nymphs or larvae in the water being fished. You can use more than one fly at the same time.

Approach

Start at the lower end of the water you wish to cover and work upstream. I like to cast up and across with relatively short casts of ten to twenty feet. The angle of your upstream cast will depend on the location of good holding water relative to where you are standing. A straight upstream cast, though still effective, is more difficult to control than a cast made across the current and upstream. Try to pick out a specific spot where you think a trout should be holding, and cast so your fly lands about ten feet upstream of that spot. Be ready to make a quick upstream mend of the fly line. This keeps a belly from forming in the line on the water and dragging your fly downstream or sideways across the current.

Most of the time, you want the indicator to drift naturally downstream without drag, just like a dry fly. As the indicator bounces along, watch for any sign of unnatural movement. Don't expect the indicator to suddenly disappear underwater. Ninety percent of the time, it will barely wiggle and may simply slow down or move slightly to the right or left. I believe many people never set the hook when they have a strike because the movement is more subtle than they expected. To help remedy this problem, if you are new to nymph fishing, try setting the hook at least once every cast. This forces you not only to pay attention, but also to set the hook when nothing very obvious has happened. You might be surprised how often a fish ends up on your line when you start setting the hook at the slightest movement of the indicator.

Once the indicator has passed the spot you picked out, follow it downstream with the point of your rod tip. As it drifts toward you, lift up the rod tip to take up the excess line on the water, then as it drifts away from you, drop your rod tip to add line to the water. When it is directly below you, or nearly so, drop your rod tip close to the water and point it at the indicator. Now you can make your next cast upstream by simply flipping your rod upstream toward the spot where you want your flies to land. In this way, you minimize false casts and avoid tangled flies and leaders. Repeat this process as you move upstream, covering all the likely holding water.

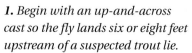

Shot and Indicator Method

1. Begin with an up-and-across cast so the fly lands six or eight feet upstream of a suspected trout lie.

2. Slowly lift the rod as you follow the indicator downstream.

3. Continue lifting line off the water to remove slack line.

4. Lift the rod tip high to maintain control as the indicator drifts downstream.

5. Pivot as the indicator drifts past you, and begin lowering the rod tip.

6. Lower the rod tip and continue pointing it at the indicator as it drifts downstream.

7. Let the line tighten downstream from you before casting upstream for your next drift.

With the line straight downstream, lift the rod and let the drag of the fly in the water load the rod for your next cast.

Aim up and across as you make your next cast without any false casting.

The shot and indicator method is effective in a variety of water types, from large rivers to . . .

. . . small streams.

Tips for Success

- Keep your casts short. It's rare that you need to make a cast of more than twenty feet. The shorter the cast, the quicker you can set the hook.
- Mend your line upstream or downstream as needed so that the indicator drifts without drag, unless you purposely want to add some action to your fly.
- Keep moving. A common mistake of beginners is to stand in one spot and continue casting for twenty or thirty minutes. If you didn't get a strike in the first ten or fifteen casts, you are not likely to get a strike in same location in the next ten or fifteen casts. After you have covered a spot with eight or ten good casts, cast farther out or take half a dozen steps upstream to cover new water.
- In most cases, your flies should drift near the bottom. If your fly does not snag or tick the bottom once in a while, add more weight to your leader. The amount of weight needed varies as you move to faster or slower water. Also make sure your indicator is far enough away from the fly to allow it to reach the stream bottom.
- Don't give up. Focus on the water where you think trout are holding, and try to visualize the underwater feeding lanes they will be using.

Hinged-Leader Method

The hinged-leader method is similar to the shot and indicator approach and can be used in many of the same water types. The main distinction of this method is that the fly hangs straight down below the indicator. With the shot and indicator method, the indicator and fly are rarely aligned vertically with each other. The hinged-leader method works particularly well in water that isn't too fast or too choppy on the surface—in other words, medium-fast runs and flats with relatively smooth surface currents. Because the nymph hangs directly below the indicator on a tight tippet, the method is also very sensitive to subtle, soft strikes.

EQUIPMENT NEEDED

Rod. A 4- to 8-weight, 8 to 9$^1/_2$ feet long, medium to slow action.

Line. A double-taper or weight-forward floating line. A double-taper has the advantage of being easier to mend.

Leader. Tapered butt section 4 to 6 feet long, plus a straight tippet section of 4X to 7X leader material 6 to 12 inches longer than the depth of the water being fished.

Indicator. Polypropylene yarn is most commonly used, but other types can be substituted.

Weight. Add shot or other weight 8 to 10 inches above the fly as needed to sink the fly to the appropriate depth. Less weight is generally needed than with the shot and indicator method.

Flies. A wide range of sizes, styles, and colors can be used, usually selected to match the dominant nymphs or larvae in the water being fished. You can use two flies, but this is less common with this method.

Approach

If you have mastered the shot and indicator method, you should have no problem with the hinged leader method, as the two approaches use nearly identical techniques. The hinged leader method is particularly good at drifting a fly through specific holding lies, so it helps to pick out lies that you want to cover. As with the shot and indicator method, position yourself down and across from the area you've selected to fish. Make your cast six to ten feet upstream of the area so your fly will have time to sink to the proper depth before it reaches the prime spot. The indicator should be directly above the fly and drifting at the same speed as the current, and the fly should be drifting naturally near the bottom if your tippet length is correct.

Mending line is often necessary to keep the indicator and fly drifting at a natural speed. Without mending, a belly often forms in your line, which creates drag on your indicator. Think of the indicator as a dry fly, and your mending is to prevent any drag of this fly on the surface. The direction

Hinged-Leader Method

(Note: The X in the following photos shows the position of the strike indicator.)

1. The hinged-leader method works particularly well in smooth flats. Begin with an up-and-across cast.

2. Follow the indicator downstream while raising the rod tip.

3. Lift as much line off the water as possible without moving the indicator.

4. *As the fly drifts below you, turn and lower the rod tip.*

5. *Continue lowering the rod as the fly drifts downstream.*

6. *End with the line almost straight below you, and make your next cast upstream without any false casts if possible.*

With the hinged-leader method, your fly should be hanging straight down below your indicator as it drifts downstream.

of your mend will depend on what the current is like between you and the indicator. An upstream mend is most common, and in the course of a single cast, you may need to mend several times to keep everything floating naturally.

While watching for drag, don't forget to watch the indicator for any unnatural movement. The indicator will rarely make large movements when a fish takes your nymph. Most often the movement is very slight and may be only a slight slowing or subtle shift right or left. The idea of setting the hook at some point on every cast is again a useful trick to get you into the habit of watching for the slightest change in the indicator's drift. When you do suspect a strike, set the hook with a quick downstream twitch of the rod tip. Setting the hook with this downstream motion results in a better hooking angle than if you lift the rod straight up.

After your indicator has passed over the lie you selected to cover, let it keep drifting downstream until it is almost directly below you. Even though a fish didn't take where you expected, you might get a take just about anywhere on the drift. After you have made half a dozen or so good drifts over the holding lie, pick out another location you think may hold fish and begin working your fly and indictor over that spot. Continue with this approach as you work upstream through the run or flat.

Tips for Success
- Identify a specific spot where you think a fish should be holding, and fish to that spot. If a fish doesn't strike where you expected one, keep following the indicator with your rod tip as it moves downstream.

- Strikes will generally be very subtle. If you are having a hard time judging what a strike looks like, try setting the hook at least once on every cast.
- Cover the water thoroughly, but don't stay in one place too long. If you've fished a stretch of water without success but feel confident it holds fish, try a different fly pattern or depth.
- If you don't see fish actively feeding, drift your nymph right off the bottom. If you aren't feeling the fly hit the bottom occasionally, you probably need to add some weight, lengthen your tippet, or both. The most common mistake anglers make with most nymph-fishing methods is not getting their flies deep enough.

Brooks Method

Charlie Brooks was the epitome of western fly fishers—innovative, observant, and independent. His books, written from the late 1960s through mid-1970s, still provide some of the best information for fishing western rivers. Charlie called West Yellowstone home for most of his fishing years, and he became an intimate observer and skilled angler on the many rivers that surround the town. With its mountainous terrain, high elevation, and prodigious snowfall, the area has many large, swift rivers with deep runs that hold some very large trout. The challenge is to find a way to get a fly to their level. Charlie Brooks developed this technique to do just that. It seems appropriate to include some of Charlie's own words about his method from *Nymph Fishing for Larger Trout* (Nick Lyons Books,

1976), which should be read by anyone wanting a full understanding of nymph fishing.

It is the channels you must fish, for these boulder-filled cuts have the depth and current barriers to provide holds for trout up to five pounds, though the average is only one and a half. The water is fast, the current in the runs moves at a speed of six to eight miles per hour. The long riffles that separate the runs are also fast—too fast to allow trout to live in them, except for the rare boulders or potholes that slow the current. These are resting spots and one will occasionally find trout of three pounds in such potholes or behind the even scarcer boulders. But the fish is only passing through; he does not live there, and it is not usually worth your time to search out and fish such places.

The tackle one must use to fish the deep runs does not appeal to some—the light-tackle people especially. Such fishing requires a rod of eight or nine feet to control the drift, and with enough backbone to raise thirty feet of deeply sunken line and a weighted nymph and hurl it back upstream without false casting. False casting a heavy weighted nymph is a form of Russian roulette with eyes and ears as stakes.

Charlie goes on to describe in detail the Brooks nymph-fishing method. I have tried to capture the method accurately in my own words below.

EQUIPMENT NEEDED

Rod. A 6- to 8-weight, 8 to 9$\frac{1}{2}$ feet long, medium action, with a strong butt section.

Line. A weight-forward, high-speed full-sinking line.

Leader. 4 to 6 feet long, with a stout tippet of 2X to 3X.

Weight. Add shot or other weight to the leader 6 to 8 inches above the fly as needed to sink the fly to the bottom.

Flies. Large, heavily weighted stonefly nymphs were Charlie's favorites for the rivers he fished. He stressed matching the dominant nymph type. And when Charlie said heavily weighted, he meant it. The big stonefly nymphs he tied had several layers of lead wire wrapped under the body.

Approach

This method is designed for fast water and is ideal for fishing the bottom of swift, choppy runs three to six feet deep. The basic technique is straightforward, but it takes practice and a certain belief that it will work to pull it off successfully. Start at the top of the run you have selected and progress downstream. Cast up and across at a 45-degree angle to the current, beginning with only about ten feet of fly line beyond the rod tip. From the spot where the fly landed until it reaches a point directly in front of you is the sinking phase. Keep the rod tip pointed at the place where the line enters the water, and simply lift the tip to take up slack line as it drifts toward you. Avoid pulling out all the slack, as this will tighten the line and impede it from sinking to the bottom.

Once the line passes in front of you and begins to drift downstream from your position, you are in what Charlie calls the fishing phase. Your fly should now be drifting near the bottom at roughly the same speed as the current. Keep following the line downstream, and lower your rod tip as needed to maintain a slight droop in the line between the rod tip and where the line enters the water. At the bottom of the drift, allow the line to straighten out completely below you, and lift the rod while keeping it parallel to the water. This is very important, as this move lifts the sunken fly line up from the bottom close to the surface before you make your next cast. From this downstream position, grab the fly line with your free hand near the stripping guide, and make a single haul as you cast upstream with the rod aiming out into the stream at a 45-degree angle. As Charlie describes it: "The rod tip does not come upright or over. The cast is like a tennis backhand [or forehand, depending on the direction of the current], with the rod almost parallel to the water throughout. In essence, this is a level cast with a single haul."

After four or five drifts, increase the amount of line you are casting by four or five feet, and fish another four or five casts farther out into the channel. Continue increasing the amount of line every four or five casts until you have all the line out that you can handle. Charlie suggests that thirty feet is a reasonable maximum. At this point, take eight to ten steps downstream and begin the process again with ten feet of fly line. This methodical approach covers the water thoroughly. As the amount of line increases, you need to lift the rod tip higher to maintain control of the line as it drifts toward you. At some point, you may have the rod straight up and your arm fully extended above your head. From this position, it is virtually impossible to set the hook, but fortunately most strikes come later in the drift, when your arm and rod tip are lower.

Strikes generally feel like a hesitation in the drift. Immediately set the hook with a combined pull on the fly line and rapid upstream movement of the rod. Because of the sinking line, setting the hook needs to be a strong, vigorous action. This is another reason for using heavy tippets—a light tippet won't last long when striking hard on a big fish in fast water.

As Charlie readily admits, many people don't like this method and give up on it. If you want to fish fast, deep water effectively, however, it is hard to find a better technique.

Brooks Method

1. Begin with an up-and-across cast.

2. Follow the line downstream, keeping the rod tip pointed where the line enters the water.

3. Continue following the line downstream. You can expect a strike at any point in the drift.

4. *Drop the rod tip slightly as the line moves below you.*

5. *Strikes often come at this point in the drift, so be ready to set the hook with a pull on the line and an upstream sweep of the rod.*

6. *Let the line straighten out completely below you, then lift the rod and as much line as possible above the water before making your next cast.*

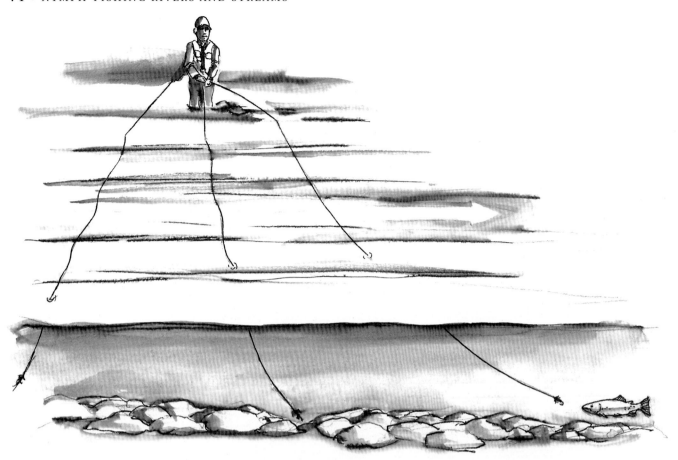

Once your fly is near the bottom, it is in the best zone for hooking fish. A strike could come at any point, but it often occurs as your line starts to tighten downstream and the fly begins lifting off the bottom.

Tips for Success

- Use a rod with enough backbone to handle a sinking line and heavy fly. This is not a method for light gear.
- Start at the top of the run and work downstream. Begin with short casts and gradually lengthen your line up to thirty or forty feet, or the amount you can comfortably handle.
- Select a fly that represents natural nymphs in the stream, and use enough weight to sink it quickly to the bottom.
- Set the hook with an upstream sweep of the rod tip and simultaneous pull on the line.
- Wade carefully. This method puts you in fast water with a bottom of large rocks—treacherous wading conditions. Use a wading staff, don't wade deeper than you feel comfortable, and pay attention to the water below you. Avoid wading above water you couldn't swim out of should you fall in, such as a set of rapids.

High-Sticking and Czech Methods

I've lumped the high-sticking and Czech methods together because they are used in similar types of water and overlap considerably in how they are performed. Use these methods in moderately deep, two- to six-foot riffles and runs with a medium current and a bottom with large cobble and boulders. Such conditions produce pocket water, still areas in front of and behind boulders, as well as deep slots between boulders and depressions along the bottom protected from the current. These waters hold a lot of good trout, but fish rarely show themselves in these areas, and many anglers pass them by because they aren't sure how to fish them. Once you learn these nymphing techniques, however, you will discover just how productive they can be.

EQUIPMENT NEEDED

Rod. For high sticking, a 4- to 7-weight, $8^{1}/_{2}$ to 10 feet long, medium-fast action, with a sensitive tip. For the Czech method, a 4- or 5-weight, 9- to 10-foot, medium-fast action.

Line. A double-taper floating line.

Leader. Tapered or straight leader $7^{1}/_{2}$ to 9 feet long, with a 3X to 6X tippet, depending on the size of fly or flies being used.

Weight. Add shot or other weight to the leader 6 to 8 inches above the fly as needed to sink the fly to the bottom.

Flies. One or two, sometimes three, flies that represent the dominant nymphal forms in the water being fished.

Approach for High Sticking

Select a pocket or current seam around a boulder or large cobble that looks like good holding water for trout, and approach the area carefully from below and off to one side until you are within a short cast, ten to fifteen feet. Make a simple lob cast five to ten feet above the area you have selected. As your line and fly drift downstream toward you, lift up your rod tip just high enough to take up the slack line. Avoid lifting up too much line and pulling on the leader, which would lift up the fly from the bottom or prevent it from sinking. As the line and fly pass in front of you and start drifting downstream, drop your rod tip to extend the line on the surface. Once the line has straightened out below you, make another lob cast upstream and repeat another drift through the same water. Make six to ten casts through the same area before selecting another pocket or slot to fish. When fishing pocket water around a boulder, drift your fly through the current seams on both sides and the quiet water in front of and behind the boulder.

This method is most effective when casting a short line. As you extend the length of your cast, you must lift your rod tip higher to take up the slack. At some point, you won't be able to lift high enough to remove all the slack. This is the maximum length of line you can effectively fish. Short casts also make detecting a strike and setting the hook much easier and therefore more effective. Detecting a strike with this method is done mostly by feel, so you need to maintain a straight line between the rod tip and fly, with some tension on the line. Any slack in the line or leader prevents you from feeling subtle takes as your fly drifts downstream. If your nymph is not reaching the bottom, you can increase its depth by casting closer to straight upstream, which reduces tension on your leader and line and allows your fly to sink more quickly; adding more weight to your leader; and increasing the length of your leader. Conversely, if your nymph is sinking too quickly and constantly getting hung up on the bottom, cast at more of an angle across stream, take weight off your leader, or shorten your leader. Any combination of these three adjustments can be used to fine-tune how deep your nymph sinks.

Tips for Success for High Sticking

- Get as close as you can to the water you wish to fish without spooking the fish. Approach from downstream to minimize this risk.
- Don't false-cast. When casting only ten or fifteen feet of line, you can easily make a lob cast up and across

Use short casts with the high-sticking method so there is little or no slack line between the rod tip and fly. This allows you to feel subtle strikes as your fly drifts downstream.

High-Sticking Method

1. Begin with a short lob cast upstream and across. This method is most often used in pocket water around boulders.

2. Follow the line downstream while you lift the rod tip high to take up slack and maintain control.

3. Continue following the line downstream with the rod.

4. *Begin dropping the rod tip as the line moves below you.*

5. *Continue dropping the rod tip. Be ready for a strike at any time.*

6. *Let the line straighten out completely below you before making another lob cast upstream.*

and above your target area. False casting may disturb the surface and scare fish or get your leader and fly tangled.

- Work through specific areas where you suspect fish to be holding. In fast, turbulent water, fish usually won't move far to take a fly, so you need to put your nymph right in front of the fish. And when you hook a fish, pay close attention to the kind of water—depth, velocity, and habitat—it was in. With this information clearly in mind, you can select similar water more easily, greatly increasing your chances of finding more fish.
- Make sure you fish deep enough. If your nymph isn't hitting the bottom occasionally, make adjustments to fish deeper.

Approach for Czech Nymphing

I've seen this technique referred to as both Czech and Polish nymphing, so perhaps it should be called Eastern European nymphing. This method has been used for many years in Europe but is just starting to gain popularity in the United States. Though it is similar to high sticking in a number of ways, there are several significant differences in how you rig and fish the leader and flies.

The method always uses at least two and usually three flies; check local fishing regulations to make sure fishing multiple flies is legal. With three flies, the heaviest one is in the middle. With two flies, the fly at the very bottom of the leader, called the point fly, should be the heaviest and needs to be weighted sufficiently to sink quickly to the bottom. The heavy fly can be selected to imitate a natural nymph, but its main purpose is to provide the weight needed to sink the other flies quickly to the bottom. The

others are typically smaller and lighter and should imitate one of the abundant naturals in the stream, usually a mayfly nymph or caddisfly larva.

The flies are attached to a leader constructed of three segments of straight leader material. A typical configuration would be 3 feet of 3X, 4 feet of 4X, and 4 feet of 5X leader material joined with triple surgeon's knots or blood knots, with a tag of about 12 inches left hanging for attaching the dropper flies. This creates a 9-foot leader with two droppers for fishing three flies. You can also use a single dropper for fishing two flies. In this case, use only two leader segments, such as 6 feet of 3X and 4 feet of 4X. The reason for using straight leader material instead of a standard tapered leader is that the finer-diameter straight leader sinks quicker than a thicker tapered leader. You can adjust the size of the leader material used depending on the size of your flies and the fish you are catching. With smaller flies and fish, you might use three segments of 4X, 5X, and 6X. With larger flies and fish, segments of 3X, 4X, and 5X might prove best.

This method requires very little casting, but you need a long, sensitive rod to cover the water and detect strikes. Pick out a likely holding spot, and approach it from downstream just as you would with the high-sticking method. With only about two feet of fly line beyond your rod tip, make a simple flip or lob cast upstream so your flies land several feet above the spot you selected to fish, again similar to high sticking. Now things change. Instead of lifting up your rod tip as the flies drift downstream, keep it just a foot or two off the water. After a brief pause to allow the flies time to sink close to the bottom, begin moving the rod tip downstream slightly faster than the current. This positive drag downstream is the key to this technique. When done correctly, your flies should be drifting close to the bottom but moving downstream

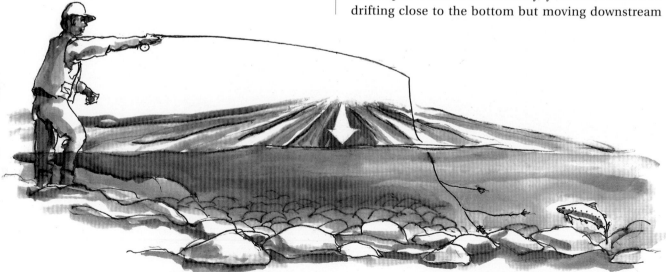

Keep your rod parallel with the water's surface as you lead your flies downstream slightly faster than the current. The tension on your line and leader allow you to detect very soft strikes.

Czech Method

1. Begin with a short flip cast upstream and across from your position.

2. Keeping most if not all of the fly line off the water, pull the line downstream slightly faster than the current. You should have enough weight on your flies and leader that they still reach the bottom.

3. Continue leading the flies downstream with the rod.

4. As the line moves downstream, you can guide it through probable fish lies.

5. Let the line drift below you and straighten out downstream.

6. Drop the rod tip and get ready to make another flip cast upstream.

slightly faster than the current. You should also have positive tension on the line and leader as you move your rod tip downstream. It is this tension that allows you to feel subtle strikes before you ever see the line move. Some anglers also believe that the movement of nymphs downstream slightly faster than the current triggers fish to strike.

Once your rod is pointing downstream, allow the line and leader to straighten out below you, and then make another little flip cast upstream. Continue until you've made half a dozen good drifts through the selected area, then move upstream or slightly farther out into the channel and cover another potential fish lie.

If your flies constantly hang up on the bottom, use lighter nymphs or move your rod tip downstream slightly faster. Conversely, if you don't feel your flies hit the bottom occasionally, switch to heavier flies or slow your downstream movement of the rod tip. One of the keys to this technique is fine-tuning the speed at which you move your rod tip downstream.

Tips for Success for Czech Nymphing

- This method works best in runs and riffles two to six feet deep with a medium current speed. Pick specific spots where you think fish should be holding, and work these locations.
- Use flies that imitate the dominant type of naturals.
- With a three-fly setup, put the heaviest one in the middle.
- Keep the rod tip near the surface of the water as you move it downstream slightly faster than the current.
- When you feel a slight tug, set the hook with a quick downstream twitch of the wrist. Don't set the hook aggressively, especially if using light tippet material.
- Keep moving upstream, covering all likely looking water. After six to ten good drifts through an area, move to another.

Sawyer Method

Frank Sawyer, a well-known English fly fisherman, developed this method specifically for fishing nymphs in the clear spring-fed chalkstreams of southern England. It is designed for fishing nymphs to trout you have actually spotted feeding, either near the bottom or anywhere below the surface. Though it was developed for spring creeks, the method can be used in any stream where you can spot fish feeding and wish to present a nymph to them. Because you need to see the fish for this method, it works best in relatively shallow, one- to four-foot, slow-flowing flats with a calm, smooth surface.

EQUIPMENT NEEDED

Rod. A 3- to 5-weight, $7^1/2$ to $9^1/2$ feet long, medium-fast action, with a sensitive tip.

Line. A double-taper floating line.

Leader. Tapered leader 9 to 12 feet long, with a 3X to 6X tippet, depending on the size of the fly being used.

Weight. Usually none. It is important, however, to get your nymph to the same depth as the fish, so occasionally, especially when fishing very small nymphs, you may need to add a split shot or other weight the leader 8 to 10 inches above the fly.

Flies. A single fly selected to imitate the nymph being eaten by the trout observed feeding. To be sure you are using the right fly, you need to spend some time collecting and observing the natural nymphs in the stream.

Approach

The Sawyer method relies on a stealthy approach to fish you have spotted. Seeing fish is not easy, even in clear spring creeks. Even though some anglers seem to have an uncanny ability to see fish, their skill didn't just magically appear; they developed it by spending hours and hours on streams or rivers looking for fish. In the process, they discovered that you rarely see a whole fish or even the actual fish itself. Often it is only the fish's shadow that gives away its position. Looking for movement is also a key to spotting fish. It might just be a waggle of the tail, a quick side-to-side twitch to grab a drifting bug, or the mouth opening and closing to feed. Once a shadow or movement identifies the fish's location, the whole fish often materializes as if some cloaking device were suddenly turned off.

While you try to spot a fish, make sure the fish doesn't spot you. To avoid being seen, approach from straight downstream or downstream and across, and keep your profile as low as possible—including your rod. Just as you spotted the trout by its movement, seeing movement above the water alerts trout to danger, so move slowly and quietly. Think of a cat stalking a mouse. You are the predator, and the trout is the prey. If the trout sees you, it may not flee, but catching it will be all but impossible.

Once you find a fish that is still feeding, an ideal casting position is ten feet downstream and off to one side. From there, you can make an up-and-across cast so that your fly lands several feet above the fish. The exact distance you should cast above the fish depends on the current speed, the weight of your nymph, and how deep the fish is feeding. You want to place the fly far enough upstream that it has time to sink to the level of the fish but not deeper. Only practice will teach you how far is far enough.

Sawyer Method

1. Spotting feeding fish is part of the excitement of the Sawyer method.

2. Don't start casting immediately. Observe how and on what the fish is feeding. In this case, the trout is feeding just below the surface on rising PMD nymphs.

3. Approach carefully, trying to keep the trout from seeing you. Approaching from downstream is usually your best bet.

4. *Make your cast above the trout with a careful presentation.*

5. *Set the hook with a gentle lift of the rod tip and be ready for a strong run. Then hang on!*

Your cast upstream also must avoid spooking the fish. A 3- or 4-weight rod-and-line combination can be a distinct advantage for this, as the light line makes little disturbance landing on the water. If possible, use a sidearm cast to keep your rod tip low while casting. Seeing a rod or line whipping through the air will alert and spook a trout as much as clumsy wading, if not more so.

If you have successfully cast above the fish without spooking it and your fly is sinking to the proper depth toward the fish, you are 90 percent there. Now all you have to do is watch the fish, since more than likely you won't be able to see your fly. If you see the fish move slightly to one side or open its mouth at the point when you judge your fly is nearby, set the hook with a gentle lifting motion. Disturb the water as little as possible so you don't scare the fish in case it didn't take your fly. If you are lucky, you may get four or five tries at a fish before it gets suspicious.

This method requires patience and skill in spotting, approaching, and making delicate presentations to fish without spooking them. I consider a success rate of 50 percent quite good, so don't feel bad when, instead of hooking the fish, you see it dart for cover. The challenge of seeing a fish and then perfecting your ability to approach and cast to it without scaring it away is a big part of the fun of this method.

Tips for Success
- Spot fish by looking for shadows along the stream bottom or small movements of a fin or tail.
- Approach fish from downstream and stay low.
- Use a rod, line, and leader for making delicate casts with little surface disturbance.
- Cast far enough upstream to allow your nymph time to sink to the same depth as the fish.
- Watch the fish for a sign that your fly was taken, and then gently set the hook.

Leisenring Lift Method

The Leisenring lift is the namesake nymph-fishing method of James Leisenring, a renowned fly fisher of Pennsylvania trout streams in the 1930s and 1940s who regularly corresponded with G. E. M. Skues in England and became a master of the nymph on his home waters. Though Leisenring was not a prolific writer like Skues, he was a skilled observer and spent considerable time collecting and studying natural nymphs and creating fly patterns to imitate them. He also developed the understanding that a good fly pattern wasn't enough for consistent success. Besides matching a natural in size and shape, he believed that flies also had to move like the natural and create the illusion of being alive. The ability to impart lifelike action to your fly is the real key to the effectiveness of the Leisenring lift. This method works well in a range of water types. I have used it with good results in moderately fast riffles, runs, flats, and even pools.

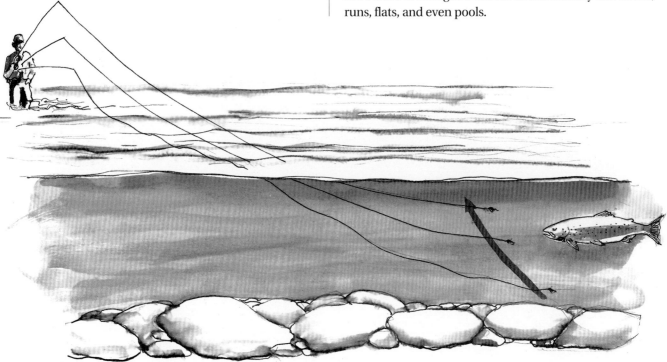

When you stop your rod and lift it slightly, your fly will begin lifting off the bottom. This action is hard for a trout to resist if the fly rises up in front of its feeding position.

Leisenring Lift Method

1. Begin by locating a fish or possible feeding position, then cast upstream far enough to allow time for the fly to sink.

2. Follow the line downstream with the rod, allowing the fly to sink.

3. As the fly approaches the trout's feeding position, stop the rod's downstream movement.

4. By holding the rod still, the line will tighten in the current, and the fly will rise toward the surface in front of the trout's feeding position.

5. Once the fly drifts past the trout's position, let it continue to drift downstream before making your next cast.

EQUIPMENT NEEDED

Rod. A 3- to 6-weight, 8 to 9¹/₂ feet long, medium action.

Line. A double-taper floating line; can also use a full-sinking or sinking-tip line.

Leader. Tapered leader 9 to 12 feet long, with a 3X to 6X tippet, depending on the size of the fly being used. Use a short leader, 4 to 6 feet long, if using a sinking-tip or full-sinking line.

Weight. Usually none. It is important, however, to get your nymph to the same depth as the fish, so occasionally, especially when fishing very small nymphs, you may need to add a split shot or other weight to the leader 8 to 10 inches above the fly.

Flies. A single fly selected to match the dominant natural nymph available to trout. To be sure you are using the right fly, take some time to collect and observe the natural nymphs in the stream.

Approach

The Leisenring lift is a frequently referenced nymph-fishing method, but the technique is often misunderstood. Too often it is described as useful only for imitating nymphs drifting near the surface just before emergence. Though it is effective for fishing flies near the surface, Leisenring used the method for fish feeding at any depth. To be effective, the fly should sink close to the stream bottom. This is revealed in his own words from his 1941 book *The Art of Tying the Wet Fly:* "Imagining we are on the stream, I cast my fly up and across about fifteen feet or more above where the big trout is located, depending on the pool and stream. The fly sinks to the bottom, progressing along naturally as I follow it with my rod, allowing no slack in the line but being very careful not to pull against it and cause it to move unnaturally." Giving your fly time to sink is an important step in this method.

Like the Sawyer method, the Leisenring lift can be used to fish to trout you have first spotted feeding. Unlike the Sawyer method, you can also use this technique effectively when you can't see the fish but have located a likely holding lie for a good trout. Cast up and across to a point far enough above the feeding fish or its suspected lie that the fly has time to sink close to the bottom before reaching the fish. After the cast, follow the drift of the fly with your rod tip so that it drifts naturally without drag, while also keeping slack out of your line. Just as your fly is approaching the trout or its lie, stop the rod tip's movement and allow the line and leader to tighten in the current. This puts tension on the line and leader, causing the fly to lift from the bottom. You can increase the speed of the lift by raising the rod tip after stopping it, but this is not always needed or appropriate. The key is activating the lift at precisely the point where the fish is holding, such that the fly rises up off the bottom directly in front of the trout. Leisenring puts it this way:

> I always fish my fly so that it becomes deadly at the point where the trout is most likely to take his food, which is usually at or close to his position in the stream. I have always contended in my mind that there is a point in fishing a fly where its appeal-efficiency is low and a point where its appeal-efficiency is high. Since my flies are tied to act lifelike and look lifelike, I fish them so that the efficiency of these qualities is at its highest when it nears and arrives before the trout for his inspection.

Trout, like other predators, respond aggressively when they see prey fleeing. The rising fly creates such an impression and triggers an almost automatic response in the trout to chase and catch the prey before it escapes. No wonder the Leisenring lift is so effective.

Because of the fly's action with this method, fish often strike hard. Strikes also occur when your line is tight and the fly is straight out or downstream from your position in the stream. Hard strikes on a tight line with the fly below you can easily result in broken tippets. To prevent a lot of lost fish, keep a loop of fly line about twelve inches long at the base of your reel, and allow this loop to slip out through your fingers when a fish strikes. This will minimize the initial shock of the strike and prevent a lot of disappointment.

Why is the Leisenring lift so commonly associated with fishing near the surface? I can think of two reasons. First, because the method depends on lifting the fly up toward the surface, many anglers focus their attention only on the "surface" part of the description. But the success of this method depends on getting the nymph below the depth of the fish before lifting it up toward the surface. As often as not, this means drifting your nymph near the bottom, which requires some combination of a weighted fly, weight on the leader, or a sinking-tip or full-sinking line, depending on the depth and water type being fished. Leisenring disliked weighted flies, as he felt the weight detracted from their action. Second, in 1971, Pete Hidy rewrote and reissued Leisenring's original book under the title *The Art of Tying the Wet Fly and Fishing the Flymph*. Hidy added information to this edition on his own method of imitating nymphs just below the surface film prior to emergence with soft-hackle emerger patterns known as flymphs. Over the years, this section on flymphs and how to fish them seems to have garnered more attention than Leisenring's other nymphing methods.

The important thing with this method is to strive to make your fly lifelike in action and present it where the fish are feeding. Sometimes that will be near the bottom, sometimes middepth, sometimes just under the surface, and sometimes on the surface.

Tips for Success
- Spot a feeding trout or pick a suspected lie for one, and concentrate on fishing to this individual fish or lie.
- Position yourself across and slightly upstream of the fish or lie you have selected.
- Cast across and upstream far enough that your nymph has time to sink slightly deeper than the fish. If you can't see the fish, assume they are near the bottom.
- Control your line to remove excess slack, and follow the drift of the fly downstream with your rod tip until your nymph has almost reached the location of the fish or its lie.
- Stop your rod and allow the current to lift the fly up off the bottom and rise up in front of the trout or its suspected lie. You may lift the rod slightly if needed to impart the proper rising action, depending on the current speed and the depth of your fly; more lift is needed in slow water than in fast.
- Keep a small loop of fly line near your reel as a shock absorber for the hard strikes that often result with this method.

Skues Method

Given the importance of George Edward MacKenzie Skues to the history and development of nymph fishing, no chapter on techniques would be complete without some discussion of his nymphing approach. When considering the nymph-fishing method employed by Skues, it is important to keep in mind the water that shaped his ideas. Skues's primary water was the River Itchen, a well-known chalkstream in southern England not far from the even better known River Test. Typical of English chalk-

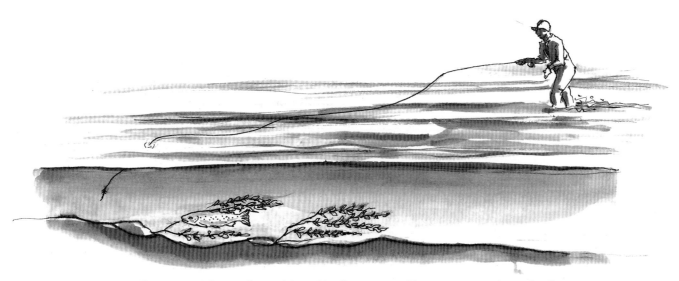

Drift your nymph over the position of feeding trout as if you are presenting a dry fly.

streams, the Itchen is a spring creek with cold, very clear water, slow currents, heavy growths of aquatic plants, dense populations of aquatic insects, and good numbers of sizable brown trout. Because of the emphasis on fishing dry flies at the time, anglers cast only to visibly feeding fish with an upstream or up-and-across presentation. It was within this setting that Skues developed patterns and tactics for taking trout feeding below the surface—a radical and controversial idea at the time.

EQUIPMENT NEEDED

Rod. A 3- to 6-weight, 7¹/₂ to 9¹/₂ feet long, medium action, with a sensitive tip.

Line. A double-taper floating line.

Leader. Tapered leader 10 to 12 feet long, with a 3X to 6X tippet, depending on the size of the fly being used.

Weight. Usually none. When using small nymphs, however, you may need to add a little weight to the leader to sink the fly even a short distance below the surface.

Flies. A single fly selected to match the natural nymph being taken by feeding trout. To be sure you are using the right fly, take some time to collect and observe the natural nymphs in the stream.

Approach

Skues devised this method for taking trout on clear, slow-flowing chalkstreams or spring creeks. Therefore, it works quite well on slow-flowing spring creeks in America as well. The method isn't limited to spring creeks, however, though it is best suited to water with a slow to moderate current speed and a relatively smooth, nonturbulent surface—in other words, pools, flats, and gentle runs.

Skues Method

1. The Skues method is good when you encounter smooth surface currents and feeding trout. Position yourself to the side and slightly downstream from a feeding trout, and cast above the fish as when presenting a dry fly.

2. *Drift the fly over the feeding trout without drag.*

3. *Watch the point where the leader goes underwater for any sign of a strike.*

4. *Once the fly has passed the trout's position, carefully lift the line off the water and make another cast.*

The other characteristic of English chalkstreams that works to the advantage of this method is their rich populations of insects. As a result, there are frequent periods when nymphs drift in the current near the surface, especially preemergent nymphs prior to a hatch. The fact that fish feeding on preemergent nymphs ignore dry flies, even when adults are on the surface, led Skues to imitate the nymph below the surface film. Though such a concept seems commonplace today, it was a radical idea in England in the early 1900s, a time dominated by the Halford dry-fly-only philosophy. Basically, Skues discovered that imitative nymph patterns presented below the surface to fish feeding during a hatch often perform much better than a dry fly—just as true today as it was a hundred years ago.

Though Skues used nymph patterns, his method is very similar to dry-fly fishing. When you come across a hatch where it appears that fish are surface-feeding on newly emerged adults but are taking preemergent nymphs below the surface, the trout will be every bit as selective to the nymphs underwater as they are to the adults on top, so the first step is to select a nymph pattern that matches the size, shape, and general color of the naturals. Position yourself across and downstream from the feeding fish, and cast upstream and across so your nymph is a few inches deep and drifting naturally without drag as it approaches the trout. Let the fly continue to dead drift, and watch for any surface disturbance as the fish turns to take the fly. An upstream mend is often needed to prevent drag. That's it. It's a simple method but effective. More than anything, it requires knowing what the fish are feeding on and a good presentation that doesn't spook the fish.

With the Skues method, the nymph is fished dead drift with no additional action. The method of fishing flymphs described by Leisenring and Hidy is nearly identical, except that you stop the drift of the fly as it nears a feeding fish so the fly rises to the surface. Leisenring corresponded regularly with Skues, so it shouldn't be surprising that there are similarities between the two methods. The added action supplied by Leisenring is certainly effective in many situations but not all. Which method should be used depends largely on the type of insect hatching. The nymphs of most mayflies and midges, dominant on English chalkstreams, drift with little action near the surface during emergence and are imitated well with a dead drift presentation. In contrast, caddis pupae, abundant in most American trout streams, rise quickly to the surface during a hatch, so adding a rising motion to your fly imitates the natural. Deciding which method to use is therefore a matter of understanding the action of the natural: When the natural drifts quietly near the surface, use the Skues method; when it rises actively to the surface, use the Leisenring lift.

Tips for Success

- Use light lines and tippets to avoid scaring fish feeding near the surface. Take the same care you would for approaching any surface-feeding fish.
- Cast upstream of feeding fish so the fly sinks a few inches to a foot below the surface.
- Mend line so you get a good drag-free dead drift presentation.
- Watch the surface for some disturbance when a fish takes your fly.

Wet-Fly Swing Method

In many ways, the wet-fly swing is an older version of the Leisenring lift, and its effectiveness also stems from the action imparted to the fly. This method has been around for at least a hundred years. I would also guess that just about everyone who has cast a fly in a stream has caught a fish using this method, whether intentionally or not. I'm referring to the situation where you are fishing a stretch of water, carefully covering feeding fish or suspected lies of fish, using a dry fly, wet fly, or nymph without success. At some point, you ignore your line and the fly swings downstream unattended, when suddenly, out of the blue, *whack!* A fish is off with your fly. Unknowingly, you fished your fly with a wet-fly swing and triggered a strike. When this happens to me, I first look to make sure no one saw it, then I give myself a pat on the back for being such a skillful angler.

This method works in all types of water and streams. It also works with imitative flies during a hatch or attractor-type flies when nothing is happening. You can cover a lot of water quickly, so it is a good searching tactic when you are having a hard time locating fish. No method is a sure thing, and a wet-fly swing won't always work. When fish are holding close to the bottom, for example, other methods will be much more effective. Still, you want to use this method from time to time, even if by accident. Besides taking trout, the wet-fly swing is often used when fishing for steelhead or Atlantic salmon.

EQUIPMENT NEEDED

Rod. A 3- to 6-weight, $7^1/2$ to $9^1/2$ feet long, medium action.

Line. A double-taper or weight-forward floating line.

Leader. Tapered leader 10 to 12 feet long, with a 3X to 6X tippet, depending on the size of the fly or flies being used.

Wet-Fly Swing Method

1. Begin with a down-and-across cast.

2. Follow the line downstream with the rod tip.

3. Make an upstream mend to keep a belly from forming in the line.

4. *Keep following the line downstream.*

5. *If necessary, make another upstream mend.*

6. *Let the line straighten out below you completely. Be ready for strikes as the fly comes up to the surface.*

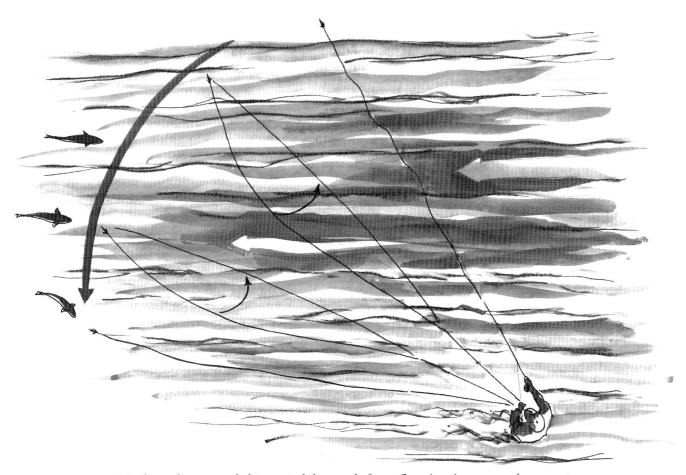

Mend your line as needed to control the speed of your fly as it swings across the current.

Weight. Usually none. When using small flies, however, you may need to add a little weight to the leader to sink the fly even a short distance below the surface.

Flies. A single fly or two-fly combination can be used. When insects are hatching, select a fly that matches the natural being taken by feeding trout. Attractor patterns can be effective when there is no insect activity.

Approach

The wet-fly swing is fished with an across-and-downstream presentation. This means you should position yourself upstream and to the side of the water you wish to cover. Cast your fly straight across or across and slightly downstream. Depending on the type of water you're fishing, a belly usually starts forming in the fly line shortly after it lands on the surface. Make a mend either upstream or downstream to remove this belly of line and keep your fly drifting naturally downstream while following your line and fly with the rod tip. Occasionally, mostly when fishing slow water, you may want to increase the speed of the fly. You can do this by making a downstream mend, which increases the size of the belly of line on the water and speeds up the fly's drift downstream.

Once the line passes about a 60-degree angle downstream, tension from the current will begin swinging your fly across the stream. As the fly comes across the water, keep your rod pointed at it. Continue to let the fly swing until it is straight below you. At this point, don't immediately pick up the fly for another cast. Let it hang in the current for a few seconds first, as fish sometimes follow the fly across the stream before finally deciding to strike. Start with short casts and progressively lengthen them to completely cover the water. You can also target particular hot spots by swinging the fly in front of features such as undercut banks, boulders, and logs.

Strikes may come at any point in the drift, but they usually occur when the fly begins swinging in the current. Because you have a tight line and the rod is pointed downstream, do not make a hard strike when a fish takes, which will almost always result in a missed fish or broken tippet. Instead, keep a short loop of fly line about twelve inches long at the base of the reel. Then when you see or feel a strike, let go of this loop of line and make a quick but easy twitch of the rod tip sideways toward the bank on your side of the stream. This ensures that the fly is in the fish's mouth before you strike, and the sideways twitch pulls the fly into the corner of the trout's mouth. After the strike, be prepared for a quick run by the fish downstream, so don't clamp down on the line with your fingers. Let the fish take line off the reel or you will quickly break it off, especially if it is a good fish.

Tips for Success
- Position yourself upstream and across from the water being fished.
- Cast straight across or across and slightly downstream. Begin with short casts and lengthen them to thoroughly cover the water.
- Mend your line to control the speed of your fly. An upstream mend to slow the fly is usually preferred.
- Follow the fly downstream with the rod tip, and let the fly hang in the current directly below you for a few seconds before making your next cast.
- Keep a loop of fly line at the base of your reel while following the fly downstream. When a fish strikes, immediately release this loop of line and make a gentle sideways twitch with the rod tip to set the hook.
- Don't hang on to the line after setting the hook. Let the fish make a run before adding pressure and recovering line.

Hewitt Method

Edward Ringwood Hewitt's nymph-fishing ideas became well known enough that a method was named after him. Hewitt wasn't just a nymph fisherman; he is known for several innovative dry-fly patterns and techniques as well, such as the Hewitt skaters. But in 1934, he published a small pamphlet called *Nymph Fly Fishing*, which popularized the Hewitt approach to nymph fishing. The Hewitt method is best used in moderate to fast riffles one to three feet deep. The idea is to use an imitative nymph relatively close to the bottom, and then lift and dip the rod tip to cause the fly to rise up and drop back down, similarly to the Leisenring lift.

Hewitt believed that riffles held the highest concentration of nymphs and therefore were the most productive areas to fish nymph patterns. Though I agree with these basic assumptions, I don't always find the Hewitt nymphing method the most effective approach for fishing riffles. For a dead drift presentation near the bottom, I think the shot and indicator approach is more effective. But if you want to fish a nymph without an indicator and don't need to get your fly to the bottom, I would recommend giving the Hewitt method a try.

EQUIPMENT NEEDED

Rod. A 3- to 6-weight, 7 1/2 to 9 1/2 feet long, medium action.

Line. A double-taper or weight-forward floating, sinking-tip or full-sinking line, depending on the depth and speed of the water.

Leader. Tapered leader 10 to 12 feet long with floating line, 3 to 5 feet long with sinking-tip or full-sinking line. Tippet size should be adjusted for the size of the fly or flies being used.

Weight. Some added weight is usually necessary to get the fly close to the bottom.

Hewitt Method

1. Start with a down-and-across cast.

2. Follow the line downstream with the rod tip.

3. Continue following the line downstream. A strike can happen at any point.

4. As the line continues downstream, the fly will begin rising up from the bottom.

Flies. A single fly or two-fly combination can be used. When insects are hatching, select a fly that matches the natural being taken by feeding trout. Attractor patterns can be effective when there is no insect activity.

Approach

Start by positioning yourself upstream and across from the water you wish to cover. Cast across and downstream at an angle ranging from 90 degrees (straight across) to about 45 degrees downstream. Make a quick upstream mend to add some slack to the line and allow your fly to sink. Once the line tightens, either continue to let the fly swing downstream with more or less a dead drift or add action to the fly by slightly raising and lowering your rod tip. I find this method best for covering specific holding lies or for fish spotted feeding below the surface. Detecting a strike isn't a huge problem, because for most of the drift you have a tight line and can feel when a fish takes your fly. As with the Leisenring lift and wet-fly swing, strikes on a tight line can easily break your tippet if you immediately set the hook, so keep a twelve-inch loop of fly line at the base of the reel, and release it when you feel the tug of a fish. After this pause, you can set the hook with a gentle rod twitch toward the stream bank nearest you.

The problem with this method is that a down-and-across cast makes it difficult to get and keep your fly very deep, since the current is constantly pulling on the line and lifting it and the fly up toward the surface. Even with a sinking line, it is difficult to get a fly more than two feet deep with this approach. In most cases, I find other techniques, such as the shot and indicator, high sticking, or Brooks method, more effective when trying to fish a nymph close to the bottom in fast water. One situation that favors the Hewitt method is a caddis hatch when pupae are darting to the surface. A tight-line, down-and-across cast works your fly with the rising, darting motion of a natural caddis pupa and can trigger some aggressive strikes.

Tips for Success

- Stand upstream and across from the water you plan to cover. It is helpful to pick out a specific lie or feeding fish and cast so your fly covers that spot.
- Cast across or down and across, and make a quick upstream mend to help sink the fly.

- Keep your rod tip pointed at the fly as it swings downstream.
- When you feel a strike, release a small loop of fly line at the base of your reel to avoid breaking your tippet on the strike. After releasing the loop of line, set the hook with a quick, gentle rod twitch toward the nearest stream bank.

Putting the Techniques to Use

These eleven techniques will effectively fish nymphs across all kinds of streams and water types. Many of them can present flies at various depths with either a dead drift or some action. A few are designed for more narrow applications. Those best suited for getting flies to the bottom in relatively deep and fast water include the Brooks, high-sticking, Czech nymphing, and shot and indicator methods. For fishing flies closer to the surface, especially during a hatch, consider the wet-fly swing, Skues, Leisenring lift, and Hewitt methods. The biggest range of choices comes when fishing water that is moderately fast—flats, runs, and riffles—and moderately deep, two to four feet. In such water, the shot and indicator, hinged leader, Hewitt, Leisenring lift, and wet-fly swing methods can all be effective, depending on how deep the fish are feeding. When little to no feeding activity is observed, the shot and indicator and hinged leader methods are the best choices. If you see that fish are more active, the Skues, Hewitt, and Leisenring lift methods are usually preferable. The Sawyer method is limited to those waters and times when you can spot fish feeding on nymphs below the surface.

Perfecting any of these methods takes time, practice, and faith that it will work. Start by selecting three or four techniques that cover the range of depths and water types you commonly encounter in your fishing. Try them in the same water type and see which one takes the most fish, then test them again in a different water type under different conditions. Learn how your line and fly feel with each method in slightly different water types. Experiment and observe, and then adopt what works and adapt what doesn't. Just keep in mind the three keys to successful nymph fishing: Present the right fly to the right place with the right action.

CHAPTER SIX

Naturals and Their Imitations

*The primary key to success with nymphs is both precise
imitation and techniques of fishing those imitations to suggest
the underwater behavior of the naturals.*

ERNIE SCHWIEBERT, *NYMPHS*

O ver the years, anglers wanting flies that consistently catch fish have developed hundreds of nymph patterns. As a result, it can be confusing to decide which you should use to imitate a particular natural. The key to selecting any fly pattern is to match as closely as possible the following characteristics of the natural: size, shape, action, and color. Of these four factors, the first three are the most important.

Anglers often ignore the size of the natural when selecting nymph patterns. There is a strong tendency to think the bigger the nymph, the better. Most of the time, this simply isn't true. To determine the proper size pattern to use, drop your selected nymph into a dish of water next to the natural being imitated and compare their sizes. If you can't match the size exactly, choose a pattern slightly smaller than the natural rather than larger since for any given species, ongoing mortality from predation or disease results in fewer older, larger individuals and more younger, smaller ones. Trout therefore see more small nymphs than large ones. The one exception is when mature nymphs are actively emerging. At this point in the life cycle, the size of nymphs does not vary much.

After considering size, select a pattern that mimics the basic shape and action of the natural. For a fat natural, use a fat fly; for a slender natural, use a slender fly. A pattern's action is perhaps affected more by the way you

fish it, but the materials used to tie a fly make a difference as well. I almost always prefer patterns tied with soft materials that are easily activated in the water over flies tied with stiff, hard materials that may look realistic but have little or no movement.

Finally, consider the color of the pattern and how well it matches the natural. If you look at half a dozen or more nymphs of the same species from the same location, however, their colors often vary, sometimes dramatically, even among individuals on the same rock. The question then becomes which color to imitate. My approach is to use a pattern of the same general hue and brightness as the natural and not worry about matching the color exactly.

The purpose of this chapter is to make a clear connection between the major types of natural nymphs and the patterns that effectively imitate them. The following pages describe the major types of insects found in trout streams and give recommendations of nymph patterns to match them and fishing tactics to imitate their behavior. Because of the vast array of nymph patterns, no one person can have firsthand experience with the all the styles available. The patterns listed in the following pages reflect my experiences and preferences, and though I am confident that they will catch fish, don't be surprised if your favorite nymph pattern is missing. The patterns listed here are only a fraction of those used by fly fishers around the country.

Two Ephemerella *nymphs on the same rock show distinct differences in color.* DAVE HUGHES

The information that is given about the insects describes their abundance and availability to trout, typical habitat, and behavior. Simple bar graphs show each group's abundance and availability.

The first bar indicates how widely distributed the particular type of nymph is in streams and rivers across North America. *Rare* indicates that it is found only at limited locations or in certain types of streams. *Locally common* means it is common in some regions or streams in North America but absent from others. *Widespread* indicates that it occurs commonly across the entire continent.

The second bar represents the abundance of nymphs in areas where they do occur. *Low* abundance means the nymphs rarely occur in large numbers, even if they are commonly found. *Medium* indicates that they are often moderately abundant but do not frequently become the dominant nymph in a stream or river. *High* means they are often one of the most abundant nymphs in the streams or rivers they live in.

The third bar indicates the nymphs' availability to feeding trout. *Low* availability means that even if the nymphs are abundant, they are rarely available as food for trout and not often important to imitate. *Medium* means that their behavior can expose them to fish when they are abundant or emerging. *High* indicates that the nymphs are readily available to feeding trout on a regular basis and patterns that match them are often effective.

The fourth bar in all but the graphs for sow bugs and scuds refers to the availability of nymphs or pupae specifically during their emergence to adults. Nymphs that crawl out of the water before adult emergence have *low* availability to feeding trout, whereas those that emerge midchannel in the surface film have *high* availability. Nymphs that have a wide distribution, high abundance, and high availability are the most important to imitate.

After collecting naturals from your stream or river, try to match the nymph you find most abundant with one of those described in this chapter. Using the information provided, you can determine how important it is to imitate and what patterns to try. Choose a size, shape, and color similar to those of the nymphs in the stream you are fishing. With this information, you should be able to select an effective pattern and fishing strategy.

MAYFLIES: Order Ephemeroptera

The order Ephemeroptera, the mayflies, has been imitated and discussed in detail by fly fishers more than any other group of aquatic insects I can think of. The reason for all this attention from anglers seems well founded, since mayflies are common to abundant nearly everywhere trout live, and many species are readily available to feeding trout throughout the year. As a result, mayflies frequently become the most important food item for fly fishers to imitate.

Mayflies come in a great variety of sizes, shapes, and colors and live in many different habitats. They also exhibit a wide range of behaviors throughout their life cycle that affect their availability to feeding trout. This means anglers need to be familiar with many different kinds of mayflies and know how to recognize the key groups in order to choose the best patterns and tactics for imitating them. There are more than seven hundred species of mayflies in North America. Such diversity can be confusing to the angler. To simplify the situation, mayflies can be divided into four groups based on nymphal behavior: swimmers, crawlers, clingers, and burrowers. The important nymphs in each of these groups are described below, which covers the major types of mayflies you are likely to find in streams and rivers across North America.

Mayfly Swimmers

The active swimming behavior of nymphs in this group causes them to routinely end up in stream drift, where they are available to feeding trout. For this reason, mayfly swimmers are among the most important nymphs in streams to imitate. More than two hundred species of mayflies are considered "swimmers" in North America. These species fall into four major families: Baetidae, Siphlonuridae, Ameletidae, and Isonychiidae. Members of the family Baetidae are particularly important; with their widespread abundance and availability, they create a consistent food source for trout wherever water flows downhill.

Blue-Winged Olives

Family: Baetidae

Major genera: *Baetis, Acentrella, Diphetor, Procloeon, Plauditus, Pseudocloeon*

Baetis *nymph.* DAVE HUGHES

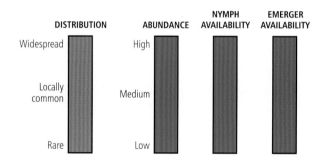

General Information. Blue-winged olive is a catchall common name for this large, complex group of mayflies consisting of nearly twenty genera and more than 150 species that all belong to one family, Baetidae. All members of this family have similar looks and behavior. Overall, these mayflies may be the most important group of aquatic insects to anyone who fly-fishes for trout. Blue-winged olives are ubiquitous, abundant, and readily available to fish day in and day out, every month of the year.

Habitat. Blue-winged olives are widely distributed across North America and are able to thrive in a wide range of habitats. This is partly because there are so many species in this group, but even individual species seem to have a broad tolerance for different habitats. From large rivers to little creeks, freestone streams to spring creeks, and slow, meandering streams to fast, steep rivers, all kinds of waters seem to be home to blue-winged olives. Nymphs can be found in large numbers in moderate to swift riffles, bouncy runs, or quiet stretches where aquatic plants are plentiful. In fact, it is rare to collect anywhere in unpolluted streams without finding at least a few, and usually a lot of, blue-winged olives.

Blue-winged olives will thrive in stream habitat like these moderate riffles and runs.

Behavior. In addition to being common and abundant, blue-winged olives seem to do whatever it takes to become food for trout. Because nymphs are active swimmers, they move around a lot, which puts them out in the water column where trout can find them. They are one of the most common aquatic insects in stream drift, so not only do they swim, but they also let go of the bottom and drift in large numbers. Mature nymphs emerge by swimming up to the water's surface, putting them directly in front of feeding trout. Most species of blue-winged olives complete several generations per year instead of just one like most mayflies, so the same species emerges two or three times a year, resulting in mature nymphs swimming up to the surface multiple times. Couple all this with the fact that most streams contain several species of blue-winged olives, and you can see why they are so important.

Size is critical when selecting patterns, and blue-winged olives are small. Mature nymphs, even for the largest species, rarely reach a size 16 hook. Most species need to be matched with flies in the 18 or 20 size range. Thus when choosing a pattern for these important mayflies, smaller is definitely better. The variety of species of blue-winged olives also means the size and color of the naturals vary by season and from one stream to the next. The only sure way to get a close match is to collect a few naturals and compare them with your flies.

Patterns. These patterns do a good job of representing the small blue-winged olive nymphs. To maintain the proper silhouette, it is important to keep the flies slender and sparse. For this reason, I rarely add weight to these small nymphs. Instead, I add split shot to my leader when I need to fish them close to the stream bottom.

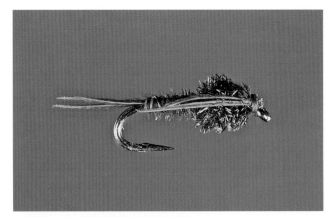

Pheasant Tail Nymph (20–16)

Krystal Flash Baetis Nymph (20–16)

Skip Nymph (20–16)

Krystal Flash Baetis Emerger (20–16)

Smurf Emerger (20–16)

Fishing Tactics. Even though many anglers find it hard to believe that such small flies fished below the surface will take trout, these patterns are incredibly successful. Effective tactics for these tiny nymphs vary with the water being fished. Since blue-winged olives live in nearly every kind of water, you'll likely need to use more than one method for fishing their imitations. The shot and indicator, hinged leader, Leisenring lift, Skues, and even Sawyer methods could all be used, depending on the type of stream and water you are fishing and whether the nymphs are actively swimming upward to emerge or drifting close to the stream bottom.

With the exception of imitating nymphs near the surface during an emergence, I find it best to fish these patterns near the bottom. Because of the flies' small size, they are never very heavy, so you need to add weight to your leader to sink them in all but the slowest of currents. Since the nymphs are active swimmers, a complete dead drift presentation isn't critical, but if you are fishing in medium to fast water, the current imparts enough action that little extra from the angler is needed. When nymphs are near the surface before emergence, added weight can be eliminated. This is a great time to fish a nymph off a short, twelve- to eighteen-inch dropper tied to the bend of a dry fly. The dry fly suspends the nymph near the surface and acts as a strike indicator, and it might actually take a fish or two in the process.

Gray Drakes

Family: Siphlonuridae
Major genus: *Siphlonurus*

Siphlonurus nymph. DAVE HUGHES

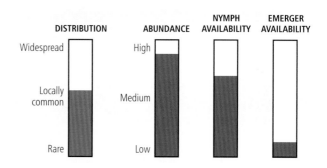

General Information. Gray drake is the most frequently applied common name, but because of color differences among species and even between duns, which are often gray, and spinners, which tend to be black, the names black drake and yellow drake are also used for members of this genus. About twenty species of *Siphlonurus* occur across North America, but they are found only in certain places. Overall, gray drakes are more common in eastern states and provinces than out west. *S. alternatus, S. quebecensis, S. minnoi,* and *S. mirus* are sprinkled across midwestern and eastern states and can be very abundant under the right conditions. Altogether, fifteen species call eastern states and provinces home. Out west, *S. occidentalis* is king, but another three species are scattered across the Rocky Mountain and southwest desert streams.

All gray drake nymphs have streamlined bodies and are moderate to large for mayflies, ranging from 3/8- to 3/4-inch long, excluding tails. Nymph colors range from light to dark gray, with a tinge of olive to pale tan with yellow undertones. Though scattered in their distribution, where they do occur they can be very abundant, providing valuable food for trout and becoming important for anglers to imitate. Gray drakes have a one-year life cycle, with emergence times spread out from May to September, depending on the species.

Habitat. Slow water with plenty of cover from wood debris or aquatic plants is the key habitat for gray drake nymphs. Many species are equally at home in streams or lakes. In streams, you will most likely find them in quiet water along the margins, in backwater areas, and around undercut banks with root tangles and wood debris.

Siphlonurus *nymphs prefer slow water with aquatic plants and wood debris.*

Behavior. The streamlined nymphs of gray drakes are excellent swimmers. Three well-developed tails with fine, interlocking hairs form an effective paddle, which the gray drake uses for propulsion by rapidly flipping the abdomen up and down like the fluke of a whale. Though the nymphs are excellent swimmers, because they live in quiet water they do not enter the drift as frequently as their fast-water relatives and therefore do not show up in fish stomachs as often. They are most vulnerable to fish when the nymphs migrate from midchannel to shoreline areas shortly before emerging into duns. Where abundant, these migrations of swimming nymphs can create a lot of excitement among hungry trout. This may be the best and last opportunity trout have to feed on nymphs, because they crawl out of the water up shoreline grasses or debris, typically at night or early morning, to emerge into duns. The only other chance for trout to feed on gray drakes is when the spinners return to lay their eggs. Spinner falls can be heavy and produce excellent surface activity.

Patterns. Though these flies are relatively large for mayfly nymphs, keep them slender to match the swimmer shape of the naturals. These patterns are often fished in relatively shallow water, so they do not need to be weighted.

Fishing Tactics. The only time I think about fishing gray drake nymph patterns is when I know mature nymphs are present and abundant. If large spinner falls of gray drakes are occurring, there might still be good numbers of nymphs near shore waiting to emerge. You can find out

Feather Duster (12–8)

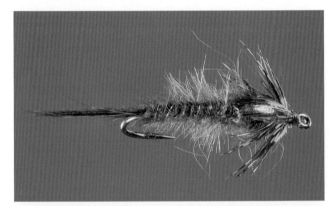

Gray Drake (12–8)

Mercer's Poxy Back (12–8)

if nymphs are abundant by collecting along the margins or backwater areas of the streams you are fishing.

When mature nymphs are present, the recommended patterns fished with a wet-fly swing can fool some large trout. Look for pools and slow-water areas with good holding lies for trout. Cast across and downstream so the current swings your nymph toward shore. Once it is close to the bank, retrieve it with short strips back upstream to make it act like a gray drake nymph struggling to get to safety. This is a great way to entice a few large trout out of their favorite hiding spots, such as undercut banks or logjams.

Brown Duns

Family: Ameletidae

Major genus: *Ameletus*

Ameletus nymph. DAVE HUGHES

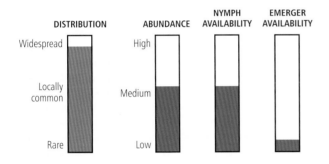

General Information. Ameletus is a diverse genus, with thirty-four species spread across North America, though twenty-six of them occur only in streams west of the Mississippi River. Despite their wide distribution, brown duns rarely occur in large numbers and are generally of minor importance to fish and anglers.

Brown dun nymphs are swift swimmers that closely resemble the nymphs of gray drakes *(Siphlonurus)*. The easiest way to distinguish the two groups is by their gills: Gray drakes have large, flaplike gills, whereas those of brown dun nymphs are slender and oval, with narrow dark bands along the leading and trailing edges. Because of the diverse number of species, brown duns occur in a range of sizes and colors. Mature nymphs typically reach 3/8 to almost 3/4 inch long, excluding tails. Nymph colors range from light tan to dark brown, with a distinct dark color band across the tails. Brown duns typically have a one-year life cycle. Given the variety of species, emergence varies from spring to fall, with peak activity common in May and September.

Habitat. Nymphs typically occur in cool mountain streams with a mixture of current speeds and substrate. I most often collect them along the edges of fast water among clean stones or where organic debris such as decaying leaves or pieces of wood have been trapped along the bottom. Different species call various types of streams home. The result is that some *Ameletus* species occur in nearly every trout stream, from small headwater streams over ten thousand feet high down to large rivers near sea level, but rarely do they occur in abundance.

You will find most Ameletus *nymphs near banks, especially where wood or vegetation is abundant.*

Behavior. Brown dun nymphs are great swimmers. When collected and placed in a tray of water, they dart around like small minnows. They feed by crawling over the surface of stones, where they scrape off diatoms—single-celled aquatic algae that form the thin, slippery film on rocks regularly cursed by wading anglers. Though brown dun nymphs are active and live on exposed rocks, their availability to trout is limited because of their rapid swimming ability and generally low abundance.

Mature nymphs move from areas of moderate current to shallow, quiet areas near shore just before dun emergence. Actual emergence takes place right at the waterline along the edges of half-submerged rocks or just above the water where nymphs have crawled up rocks, grass stems, or small pieces of wood. Because of this behavior, the availability of nymphs to trout is marginal at best during emergence.

Patterns. When tying nymphs to imitate brown duns, keep in mind that the naturals are streamlined, swift swimmers, so the patterns should be slender as well.

Near Enough (12–10)

Theo's CDC Brown Devil (12–10)

Fishing Tactics. I've collected brown duns in nearly every trout stream I've fished. That said, I have rarely needed to specifically imitate them. The reasons seem to be their low abundance and behavior that keeps them out of the mouths of feeding trout. On those rare occasions where these nymphs are concentrated and fish find them available, a wet-fly swing will probably prove most effective. These nymphs are fast swimmers, so impart a slight pulsing twitch to your rod as the fly swings across the current. Once the fly edges toward the shore, don't immediately lift it up for the next cast. Let it sit a few seconds, and then retrieve it upstream several feet with short strips and twitches.

Great Leadwings

Family: Isonychiidae
Major genus: *Isonychia*

Isonychia *nymph.* THOMAS AMES

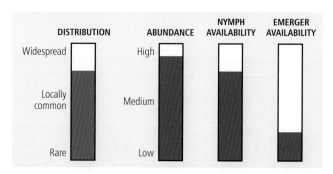

General Information. North America has seventeen species of great leadwing mayflies, also known as leadwing coachmen or slate drakes. Their distribution and abundance differ in the East and West. Throughout the East, they are widespread, abundant, and an important mayfly, but in western states, they are rarely present and of minor importance. In the few western streams where they do occur, however, they can be present in large numbers and worth imitating. These streams are mostly found in southern Oregon and in California along the Sierra Nevada.

Isonychia nymphs resemble the large swimming nymphs of *Siphlonurus* and *Ameletus* in many ways. They overlap in size, with *Isonychia* nymphs ranging from 1/2 to 3/4 inch long. In shape, they all have slender, torpedo-like bodies built for swimming, with three tails fringed with fine hairs. In color, *Isonychia* nymphs are darker, ranging from dark gray to reddish brown. The common eastern species, *I. bicolor,* has a distinct cream stripe down the middle of its thorax and abdomen. All have a one-year life cycle, with emergence spread out over the season. In the East, where *Isonychia* is most important, emergence begins in mid-May and continues sporadically all summer into October.

Habitat. Great leadwings seem happy in moderate to fast runs and riffles that bounce over large rocks and cobble. They are equally at home on small streams or large rivers where the current moves briskly. Unlike *Siphlonurus* and *Ameletus,* which avoid the main force of the current by staying near shore, *Isonychia* nymphs thrive in midchannel areas in the main current. Still, by living on large cobble, they have plenty of places to get out of the current's full force. These nymphs are such strong swimmers that they can dart from rock to rock, even upstream against the current when needed.

Behavior. Isonychia nymphs have a unique feeding approach that takes advantage of the fast water where they live. Their front legs are fringed with long hairs along the inside margins. By facing the current and spreading their front legs, the long hairs cross, forming a small basket, which functions like a net to strain plankton out of the current. Large, mature nymphs aren't shy about eating other small insects on occasion as well.

Though *Isonychia* nymphs don't avoid swift water for most of their one-year life cycle, as they approach emergence, mature nymphs seek quieter water. Sometimes nymphs move to quiet areas near shore, but they also like slow flats or pools below riffles. For actual emergence into duns, some nymphs crawl out onto protruding rocks or sticks, and others swim up to the surface film, where the duns emerge in open water. Overall, *Isonychia* nymphs offer more opportunities than the other large swimming mayflies for trout to dine on them, and they should not be overlooked on streams where they are abundant.

Patterns. Gray leadwing nymphs, though still excellent swimmers, are a bit stockier than other swimming nymphs. This means their imitations can be tied a bit fuller and less tapered from front to back. Adding weight to these patterns is also useful, since the naturals live in swift currents where sinking a fly, even a foot or two, requires weight. A beadhead added to any of these patterns can provide the necessary weight and give some action to the fly as well.

Fishing Tactics. The importance of these nymphs rises and falls with their abundance in the streams you fish. You can usually determine if they are present in good

Isonychia Nymph (10–8)

Gray Drake (10–8)

numbers by taking a quick kick sample in a moderately fast riffle. If the nymphs are present, you will see them flipping in the net like $1/2$-inch-long miniature minnows. Choose a nymph pattern of the right size, and then start drifting it close to the bottom through good trout water in the riffles and runs. The shot and indicator, high-sticking, and Czech methods can be used, depending on the specific water type. Because these nymphs are such good swimmers, add a few twitches to your drift if a dead drift approach isn't working. If you find that mature nymphs have migrated to areas near shore, cover the quiet areas along the bank before fishing farther out in the channel. Try a wet-fly swing so your fly swings downstream close to shore, and then retrieve it with short strips back up against the current.

Mayfly Crawlers

Pale morning duns, Hendricksons, sulfurs, western green drakes, flavs, mahogany duns, and Tricos are some of the best-known names in stream hatches, and they all belong to the crawler group of mayflies. These insects have attracted the attention of fly fishers for well over a hundred years and for a good reason: They excite trout into reckless feeding both under and on the surface, and they are widespread, abundant, and available.

The crawler classification has just three main families of mayflies—Ephemerellidae, Leptophlebiidae, and Leptohyphidae—but there are many important genera and species within these families. Altogether, about 220 different species of mayflies crawl along the bottom of North American streams and rivers.

The largest and most confusing of these families is Ephemerellidae. To help simplify this large family of important species, it can be divided into three subcategories based on size: small, medium, and large ephemerellids. While somewhat arbitrary, this breakdown simplifies pattern selection and fishing strategies for an otherwise unwieldly group.

Crawlers call many types of stream habitat home, including slow moving sections where selective fish and calm water make success that much sweeter.

Small Ephemerellidae: Pale Morning Duns, Hendricksons, Sulfurs

Family: Ephemerellidae
Major genus: *Ephemerella*

Ephemerella subvaria. THOMAS AMES

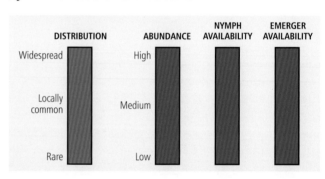

General Information. This group of mayflies is widespread, abundant, and available and ranks as one of the most important in streams throughout North America. The dominant species all belong to the genus *Ephemerella,* of which thirty-five are known in North America but only a handful are important to anglers. In western streams, one species, *E. excrucians* (formerly *E. inermis*), or pale morning duns, provides almost all the action. In midwestern and eastern streams, several important species come into play: *E. subvaria* (Hendricksons), *E. invaria* (pale evening duns), and *E. dorothea* (sulfurs).

Besides the few dominant species, numerous less common species of *Ephemerella* live in the same streams but are next to impossible for the angler to accurately identify. These lesser cousins can easily be confused with the more common species and create conflicting ideas about what the size and color of the pattern should be. The answer is simple: Use a pattern that matches the natural that is dominant in the stream on the day you are fishing. Like crawlers in general, *Ephemerella* nymphs are more rectangular in shape than the streamlined swimmers, with legs that are rather short and stout and tails fringed with fine hairs.

Habitat. Part of the reason these small ephemerellid species are so important is that they thrive in a wide variety of habitats and stream types. Nymphs do well in slow to fast currents, with substrates ranging from large cobble to small gravel, and in beds of aquatic plants or organic debris such as dead leaves and twigs. I have collected excellent numbers of *E. excrucians* from small coastal streams, large valley rivers, and gently flowing spring creeks. Some species, such as *E. subvaria* (Hendricksons), are sensitive to water quality and have declined as pollution has affected more streams throughout their range. Other species are able to tolerate some pollution and continue to produce excellent hatches.

Gentle runs and flats with a gravel bottom harbor excellent populations of Ephemerella *nymphs. This group occurs in many other types of habitat as well.* DAVE HUGHES

Behavior. The behavior of these abundant species enhances their availability to trout. Nymphs, especially those living in riffles with moderate to fast current, routinely drift in good numbers, and because they are not excellent swimmers, they take longer to get back to the bottom than swimmer nymphs. All species have a one-year life cycle, though specific emergence time varies with the species and temperature conditions of the stream; hatches will be later in colder streams.

Nymphal behavior just before and during emergence increases their availability. Mature nymphs get restless and climb up on top of the rocks or stones they normally hide under. As a result, their numbers in stream drift increase significantly. When finally ready to emerge, the nymphs let go of the bottom and swim up to the surface film. But rather than make this trip to the surface just once, they often return to the bottom for a few minutes and then make another trip up to the surface. What more could a hungry trout ask for? The nymphs of most species hang in the surface film while the duns escape their shucks and pop out on the surface. Trout often respond with classic bulging-type rises as they pluck the hanging nymphs out of the surface film. In some instances, however, the duns actually emerge from the nymphal shucks underwater while the nymphs rest on the bottom or as they swim up to the surface. In either case the duns must float a foot or more through the water before escaping to the surface. When this happens your patterns should represent submerged duns rather than nymphs.

Patterns. Nymph patterns for these small ephemerellids are some of my favorite go-to flies. I tie them with and without beadheads to fish at different depths. Though the effectiveness of these patterns increases just before and during hatches, I fish them year-round with good success.

Flashback Hare's Ear (18–14)

Beadhead PMD Nymph (18–14)

Skip Nymph (18–14)

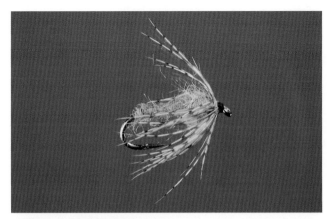

Partridge and Orange (18–14)

PMD Emerger (18–14)

CDC PMD Emerger (18–14)

Fishing Tactics. Like the small swimming nymphs of blue-winged olives, these nymphs live in so many different kinds of water and streams that no one tactic will fit all situations. The type of water you are fishing and the depth you need to fish—bottom, middepth, or near the surface—determine the best nymphing method to use. When I'm imitating nonemerging nymphs close to the bottom, I find the shot and indicator approach effective most of the time. When nymphs begin emerging, however, the Leisenring lift or Skues method can be perfect. I also like to hang a nymph off a dropper attached to a dry fly during a hatch. This offers fish both an emerging nymph and a dun to choose from. When duns are emerging underwater, try a wet-fly-type emerger pattern, fished near the surface with little or no action. The wet-fly swing or Skues method can be effective here.

Medium Ephemerellidae: Flavs, Blue-Winged Olives

Family: Ephemerellidae
Major genus: *Drunella*

Drunella coloradensis *nymph.* DAVE HUGHES

Drunella lata *nymph.* THOMAS AMES JR.

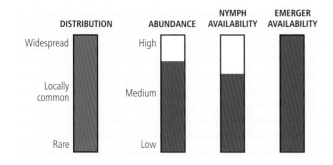

General Information. The genus *Drunella* is widespread across North America, with fifteen species occurring in streams with moderate to fast cold water flowing over clean gravel or cobble. There is a distinct East-West divide, however, in terms of species distribution. In midwestern and eastern streams, five similar-looking species can be found: *D. cornuta, D. cornutella, D. lata, D. longicornis,* and *D. walkeri.* In western streams, two species are impor-

tant: *D. coloradensis* and *D. flavilinea.* While all belong to the same genus and have many similar traits, the eastern species, matched with hook sizes 14 to 18, are distinctly smaller than their western cousins, at sizes 12 and 14. Referring to these eastern species as medium may be a stretch, but they are fatter than the small ephemerellids of the genus *Ephemerella.* All *Drunella* nymphs have over-size front legs that look like Popeye's forearms after a serious hit of spinach.

Common names also reflect regional differences. Eastern species are generally referred to collectively as eastern blue-winged olives, or simply blue-winged olives—the same common name used for the important group of swimming mayflies of the family Baetidae. Such overlap in common names occurs all too frequently and creates its share of confusion. Out west, both species are called flavs, which is short for the species name *D. flavilinea.* No matter what the name, they hatch the same, and whether you fish East or West, these are important species to imitate.

Habitat. The species of *Drunella,* East and West, prefer faster water and larger cobble substrate than those of the genus *Ephemerella.* Medium to fast riffles and runs seem to hold the best populations. The stream size or type doesn't seem to matter, as I have collected good numbers from all manner of little creeks to large rivers and spring creeks to tailwaters. In the West, *D. coloradensis* prefers colder water, predominating in streams or stream segments that remain below 60 degrees F, whereas *D. flavilinea* is more numerous in waters that regularly get above 60 degrees.

Riffles with a cobble bottom provide excellent habitat for the medium Ephemerella *species.*

Behavior. The greatest availability of *Drunella* nymphs occurs during emergence. Before this phase, nymphs do a good job of holding on to rocks and hiding in the crevices between them out of the main force of the current. As a result, they do not end up in stream drift as frequently as other mayfly nymphs. When the nymphs are abundant, however, I find a nymph pattern drifted close to the bottom a good way to catch trout in riffles and runs, especially in early morning or late evening.

Once the nymphs are mature and close to emergence, they become much more active and more frequent in the drift. Most hatches occur around midday from late spring through the summer. The nymphs become particularly active an hour or two before emergence and then finally swim clumsily to the surface, where they emerge in the film or just below it. The few hours leading up to the hatch is an excellent time to fish nymphs from the bottom up to the surface.

Patterns. These are some of my favorite searching nymph patterns in streams that have good populations of *Drunella* mayflies. Size and color of the naturals vary depending on the species present, so it helps to collect a few before selecting a fly.

Olive Beadhead Hare's Ear (14–10)

Fishing Tactics. Prior to emergence, the nymphs spend most of their time in riffles and runs and live close to the bottom. Therefore, you need to use nymphing tactics that

Flashback Beadhead Hare's Ear (14–10)

Pheasant Tail (14–10)

will get your fly to the bottom effectively. The high-sticking, Czech, hinged-leader, and shot and indicator methods can all be effective, depending on the specific water type being fished. Once emergence starts, methods like the Leisenring lift work well before serious dry-fly action begins. Many fish focus their feeding on nymphs just below the surface even when duns are drifting downstream in large numbers. Though it may be hard to resist, don't switch to dry flies too soon.

Large Ephemerellidae: Western Green Drakes

Family: Ephemerellidae
Major genus: *Drunella*

Drunella grandis *nymph.* DAVE HUGHES

Drunella doddsi *nymph.* DAVE HUGHES

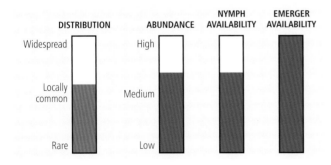

General Information. The large Ephemerellidae is a distinctly western group of mayflies consisting of three species that range throughout the Rocky Mountains west to the Pacific: *D. doddsi, D. grandis,* and the less common *D. spinifera.* To make matters a little more confusing, *D. grandis* is divided into three subspecies: *D. grandis grandis, D. grandis ingens,* and *D. grandis flavatincta.* You don't need to worry about these taxonomic fine points, however.

All you need to know is when these large, juicy mayflies are present and being eaten by trout, because when they are, you can experience some mighty exciting fishing.

These species of *Drunella* look similar to the medium Ephemerellidae except for their size. Mature nymphs reach almost 3/4 inch long, excluding tails, and their bodies are quite robust. *D. spinifera* and *D. grandis* sp. also have pronounced spines growing off their head, thorax, and abdominal segments. Nymphs of *D. doddsi* have no spines, but instead have a unique pile of fine, dense hairs covering the underside of the abdomen. These hairs function like one side of a Velcro strip, providing a tenacious grip on bottom rocks. The duns and spinners of all three species are so similar in size, color, and shape that the only way to determine which is which is to collect emerging nymphs, which can be identified rather easily by the above characteristics, or get out a microscope and look at the shape of the male reproductive structures. It may sound kinky, but it's what entomologists do for fun.

Habitat. Though these nymphs are widely distributed within their western home range, their abundance varies considerably from stream to stream, and it's difficult to know why. Some streams have become famous because of their abundant western green drake hatches, such as the Railroad Ranch section of the Henry's Fork. When present, the western green drake nymphs are usually found in fast riffles and runs with large cobble substrate. In cold spring creeks, *D. grandis* and *D. spinifera* nymphs also occur in gentler currents where aquatic plants are abundant or wood debris is prevalent. It is common to find all three species together in the same stream, often on the same rock. Once mature, nymphs migrate to slower water along the margins of riffles before beginning emergence.

Swift riffles with a cobble bottom are preferred by western green drakes.

Behavior. For the most part, these large nymphs are not readily available to trout until they are close to emergence. Though they live in fast water, they have a tight grip on the bottom and are able to find areas on large cobble out of the current. Still, when the nymphs are abundant and well developed, they can end up in the drift, where opportunistic trout find these large, juicy morsels hard to resist. The availability of nymphs increases when they begin migrating to slower water prior to emergence. Once ready to emerge, nymphs may drift some distance along the bottom before beginning to swim clumsily toward the surface. Dun emergence occurs underwater or in the surface film. Nymphs in this stage are most vulnerable and most important to imitate.

Patterns. Large, bulky nymph patterns do a good job of imitating the fat naturals. They should be weighted because of the fast-water habitat and bottom-dwelling nature of the nymphs. Colors are usually quite dark, almost black, though in some streams the nymphs are light olive to gray. Charlie Brooks's Ida May is one of my favorite nymph patterns for these big western green drakes. Also carry a few wet-fly emerger patterns to imitate those duns that escape from the nymphs under the surface.

Beadhead 20-incher (12–8)

Fishing Tactics. Drifting big nymphs along the bottom in fast water is the general approach for fishing western green drake nymphs. If the water is very deep, greater than three feet, the Brooks method works well. The high-sticking, Czech, and shot and indicator methods can also work, depending on the specific stream conditions where you are fishing. Once the nymphs start emerging, you may want to switch tactics, especially if duns are emerg-

Possie Bugger (12–8)

Ida May (12–8)

CDC Green Drake Emerger (12–8)

ing below the surface and floating up to the top. If that's happening, put on an emerger pattern and fish it with a Leisenring lift in quieter water along the margins of riffles and runs or in flats downstream of them. Using a bushy dry fly with an emerger hanging below on a dropper is also a good method when you aren't sure whether fish are taking emergers or drys.

Mahogany Duns

Family: Leptophlebiidae
Major genus: *Paraleptophlebia*

Paraleptophlebia nymph. DAVE HUGHES

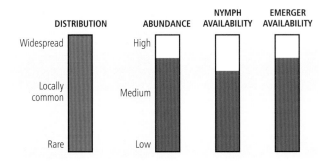

General Information. Mahogany duns look nothing like the previously discussed crawlers, yet they still belong to this class of mayflies because of the crawling behavior of the nymphs. Rather than stocky and robust, *Paraleptophlebia* nymphs are slender and delicate looking. They range from small to medium, sizes 18 to 12, and they vary in color from dark chocolate brown to tan. Mahogany dun is a frequently used common name for this group; other names include blue quill, blue dun, and slate-winged mahogany dun. The nymphs are often called forked-gills because of their distinct tuning-fork-shaped gills.

   Paraleptophlebia is a diverse genus, with thirty-nine known species widely distributed across North America. Abundant populations occur in both eastern and western streams, but the major species differ. The dominant species in the East are *P. adoptive, P. mollis,* and *P. debilis,* and in the West, *P. gregalis, P. memorialis, P. debilis,* and *P. bicornuta.* Given their diversity, range, and abundance, you will likely need to imitate these mayflies at some point during the season.

Habitat. Mahogany dun nymphs shift their habitat preferences as they mature. Young nymphs prefer moderate to quick riffles with a rocky bottom, where fine organic debris accumulates in the cracks and crevices between rocks. The debris provides both food and shelter for the small, delicate nymphs. As they mature, they move to gentler water, usually close to the riffles they inhabited as youngsters. Though living in quieter water, nymphs still look for organic debris such as piles of decaying leaves and aquatic plants for food and shelter. While most species can adapt to a wide variety of stream types, I generally find better populations in lower-gradient, more gently flowing streams than in steep rivers with strong, heavy currents. Spring creeks, with rich growths of aquatic plants, also harbor large populations.

Gentle runs and flats with organic debris on the bottom provide excellent habitat for Paraleptophlebia *nymphs.*

Behavior. Paraleptophlebia nymphs are feeble swimmers that spend most of their time hiding and feeding in organic debris. This behavior reduces their exposure to stream drift for most of their one-year life cycle. But as with most other mayflies, when the nymphs reach maturity and are ready to emerge, they expose themselves to the current in their effort to reach the water's surface where the duns escape. Their ability to swim isn't any better as mature nymphs, so when they let go of the stream bottom, they drift some distance before reaching the surface. Once at the surface, nymphs often hang briefly in the film before the duns emerge. This sequence creates excellent opportunities for trout to zero in on rising nymphs and emergers in the film. Some species crawl up plants or debris to within a foot or so of the water's surface, where the dun emerges underwater and then drifts up to the surface. In nearly all cases, nymph and dun activity is focused in quiet flowing areas near shore or slack water such as flats and eddies.

Patterns. Patterns for *Paraleptophlebia* nymphs should be slender and sparse. I rarely weight them, as they are often fished in slow water where little weight is needed. The color of nymphs varies little among species, but they can range in length from size 18 to 14, so check the size of the naturals before selecting a pattern. It is good to carry some emerger patterns along with nymphs, since both may be needed in the early stages of a hatch.

Copper John (18–14)

Trina's Bubbleback Emerger (18–14)

Fishing Tactics. Because most feeding activity occurs in quiet water, nymphing tactics that allow delicate presentations are best. The hinged-leader method works

CDC Pheasant Tail Beadhead Emerger (16–14)

Brook's Sproat Emerger (16–14)

Lawson's Floating Nymph (16–14)

well when fish are taking nymphs drifting close to the bottom or middepth. When the nymphs have made it closer to the surface, try the Sawyer or Skues method. These techniques were devised for fooling selective trout in quiet spring creeks, which closely matches many mahogany dun fishing situations. Part of the excitement of a mahogany dun hatch is that you can often spot trout feeding in the quiet water where hatches occur, and then stalk and cast to individual fish. This becomes a test of your ability to approach a feeding trout and make a successful presentation. And the bigger the trout, the more exciting this test becomes.

Tricos

Family: Leptohyphidae
Major genus: *Tricorythodes*

Tricorythodes *nymph.* DAVE HUGHES

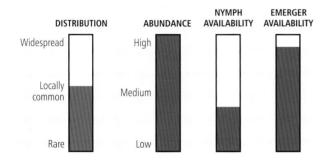

General Information. Species of the genus *Tricorythodes* are referred to as Tricos for short, though I've heard anglers use many other names for them while fishing during their famous hatches and spinner falls. During Trico hatches, the naturals occur in huge numbers, causing trout to feed heavily and selectively and driving anglers crazy trying to fool feeding trout.

Tricos occur across the continent but only in streams with the right conditions. When conditions are right, the numbers of these little mayflies can be truly amazing. The major species in midwestern and eastern streams are *T. minutus, T. stygiatus,* and *T. allectus;* in western streams, *T. minutus* is the most common and abundant. The shape, color, and manner of these species are similar, so knowing which is present is not something to be concerned about. Carefully matching the size of your pattern to the natural, however, is important. All Tricos are small; depending on the species and stream, you will need patterns between sizes 18 and 24.

Habitat. Tricos have adapted to conditions other mayflies find unacceptable: slow-moving streams with silty bottoms. Therefore, streams with rocky riffles and runs and clean gravel bottoms—the kind of habitat we often think of as trout water—don't have good Trico populations. Instead, Tricos go for low-gradient, gently flowing streams with silty substrate and beds of aquatic plants. Many streams with this habitat get too warm for trout, so even though they may produce good Trico hatches, there are no trout to fish for. Spring creeks, however, often have excellent Trico habitat and cold water ideal for trout. This is why some of the most impressive Trico hatches happen on spring creeks, such as Silver Creek in Idaho. Many tailwater streams also produce conditions just right for Tricos and trout.

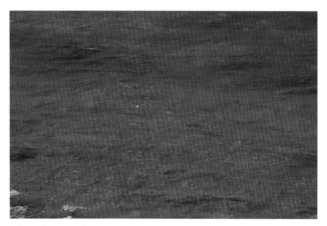

Slow flats with aquatic plants on the bottom can produce dense populations of Tricos.

Behavior. Tricos crawl quietly along in the silty, plant-covered stream bottoms they prefer. The gills on the first abdominal segment are large, triangular plates that cover all the remaining gills of the other abdominal segments and are a big reason Tricos can survive in silty streams. Covering the gills on other segments prevents silt from clogging them and reducing their ability to extract oxygen. The small size of Trico nymphs also means their demand for oxygen is small.

Because of the slow current and slow-moving nature of Trico nymphs, they are not often available to trout even when present in large numbers. Trout must wait until the nymphs leave the stream bottom and rise to the surface to emerge before getting a chance to feed on them. The problem for anglers is that this often occurs at night or very early in the morning before sunrise. If you arrive at the stream at 7 or 8 A.M., most of the duns have already emerged and are molting into spinners. Huge swarms of spinners soon form in the air, and by 9 A.M., the water is covered with spent spinners and trout are gorging on these tiny but plentiful treats. As a result, nymphs and nymph patterns are of minor consequence when it comes to fishing a Trico hatch.

The best fishing during the Trico life cycle is compressed into the final two hours, when spinners mate and lay eggs on the water. If this occurred during only a week or two each season, Trico hatches would be a much smaller footnote on the fly fisher's calendar. But in most streams, Tricos have very short life cycles, completing development from egg to spinner in just six or seven weeks, and different generations often overlap. This results in a nearly continuous emergence of adults for months. June through September produces some the best hatches and spinner falls. Some spring creeks with near-constant year-round water temperatures may have Trico hatches every month of the year.

Patterns. Because of the behavior and timing of nymph activity, nymph patterns for Tricos are of minor importance compared with dun or spinner imitations.

Fishing Tactics. If you run into a situation where fish are taking Trico nymphs, it will probably be in the early morning when female duns are still emerging. The nymphs will therefore be swimming up to the surface or in the surface film. To match this activity, fish a nymph pattern a foot or two deep or in the surface film with a dead drift. One of the easiest ways to do this is to tie a nymph on as a dropper below a dry fly. Strikes are usually very gentle, so the dry fly acts as a strike indicator and keeps the nymph suspended at the right depth. If you need to fish the nymph in the film, apply some floatant to your leader to within a couple inches of the nymph. When

Trico Nymph (24–18)

Trico Spinner Wet (24–18)

trout are ultra-selective on spinners, try a soft-hackle spinner pattern fished dead drift just below the surface. Though not truly nymph fishing, it is fishing below the surface and it works.

Mayfly Clingers

The nymphs in this group remind me of Formula 1 race cars: They are low-slung, aerodynamic, and designed for the fast lane, in this case meaning swift riffles and runs. Everything about the shape of clinger nymphs is about reducing drag. The head, which looks like a large, flat, oval plate, is wider than the thorax or abdomen, whereas the heads of all other mayfly nymphs are narrower than the other segments. Thus recognizing clinger nymphs can be quick and easy; just look at the size and shape of the head. The legs of clingers sprawl out from the body spiderlike, while the thorax and abdomen are depressed top to bottom. All of this adds up to a body that looks as if it has been run over by a car. The shape, however, is perfectly suited to cling to rocks in fast water without being washed away.

All clingers belong to a single family, Heptageniidae, which includes fourteen genera and more than 130 species. Some of the best-known mayfly hatches of the season, such as march browns and Quill Gordons, are clingers. Though there are several important hatches of clingers, all have similar behavior and can be imitated with similar tactics and patterns; you just need to adjust the size and color for the species. For this reason, I have lumped pattern and fishing information together for all clingers.

Clingers love riffle and run habitat, and so do trout. Drift your nymphs along the seams where depth or current velocities change.

March Browns, Quill Gordons, Cahills, Pale Evening Duns, and Others

Family: Heptageniidae
Major genera: *Epeorus, Heptagenia, Leucrocuta, Nixe, Rhithrogena, Maccaffertium, Stenonema, Stenocron*

Rhithrogena morrisoni *nymph.* DAVE HUGHES

Epeorus *nymph.* DAVE HUGHES

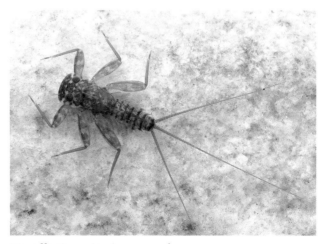

Mccaffertium vicarium *nymph.* THOMAS AMES

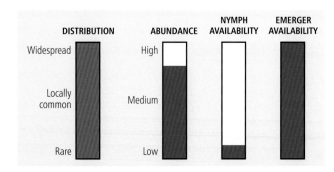

Fast water and the slower water nearby hold good numbers of clinger nymphs.

General Information. Because there are multiple genera and species of clingers, their hatches occur at various times throughout the season. In eastern and midwestern streams, the general progression of major hatches is as follows:

- Quill Gordons *(Epeorus pleuralis):* April–May
- March browns *(Maccaffertium vicarium):* May–June
- Light cahills *(Stenocron interpunctatum):* June–mid-September
- Pale evening duns *(Leucrocuta hebe):* mid-July–mid-October

The primary western clinger hatches progress in the following order:

- March browns *(Rhithrogena morrisoni):* February–May
- Pale evening duns *(Heptagenia elegantula):* mid-May–July
- Small western red quills *(Rhithrogena undulata):* mid-June–September
- Slate brown duns *(Epeorus longimanus, E. albertae):* June–September

In any healthy trout stream, these hatches overlap with a variety of other mayfly, caddisfly, and stonefly hatches. Therefore, it is critical to carefully observe exactly what trout are feeding on and how they are feeding to determine what patterns and tactics should be used.

Habitat. Because clingers prefer fast to moderately fast water in riffles and runs with a small to large rocky substrate, the size of the stream doesn't really matter, as long as it has riffles with clean gravel bottoms. Though the nymphs like to live in fast water, it is not uncommon for mature ones to migrate to more moderate currents in flats and runs below or next to riffles before dun emergence begins. Many clinger species are very sensitive to human disturbance that warms the water or causes fine sediment to accumulate on the stream bottom, so some hatches have declined dramatically in streams where logging, development, or pollution has affected the water quality.

Behavior. Clingers move effortlessly across the surface of the large rocks they call home. They feed by scraping off the periphyton, a thin layer of diatoms that grow in abundance on the surface of stones and rocks in clean streams. Periphyton also creates the slippery surface on stream rocks that we try to overcome with felt soles and studded wading shoes. Clinger nymphs may not look it, but they are extremely quick and agile at moving over the surface of submerged rocks. This was demonstrated one day while I was snorkeling in a small stream. Lying quietly in a riffle, only about a foot deep, I saw several *Epeorus* nymphs grazing on the upper surface of a stone about ten inches in diameter. It was a sunny day, and I moved my hand so it cast a shadow over the grazing nymphs. When the shadow passed over them, they disappeared under the cobble quicker than I could blink. After a few minutes, they slowly crawled back up to the top and started grazing once more. I repeated my shadow test, and again they moved to the underside of the stone so fast they seemed to vanish before my eyes. I came away with new appreciation for the agility of these little nymphs.

The ability of clinger nymphs to stick to the bottom, even in fast-water riffle habitat, keeps their numbers in stream drift low, and hence their availability to trout. It is only when they reach maturity that these nymphs become important to imitate. Most clinger nymphs swim up to the surface film, where duns escape the nymphal shuck. Occasionally duns emerge just below the surface and rise up a few inches to reach the new world of air above the water.

Patterns. All clinger nymphs have the same basic shape and behavior, so the same patterns can be used to imitate any of the various species, as long as you match the size and general color of the dominant type in the stream you are fishing.

March Brown (16–12)

A. P. Olive (16–12)

Fishing Tactics. When clinger nymphs are mature and active, they drift briefly near the bottom and then swim up to reach the surface. In most cases, they do this in riffles and runs or the flats below them. If you see fish feed-

Mercer's Poxy Back (16–12)

March Brown Flymph (16–12)

ing just below the surface, the Leisenring lift is a good approach. Position yourself so your nymph rises up right in front of a feeding trout. If fish are feeding close to the bottom, try fishing your fly dead drift along the bottom using the shot and indicator method. If you are in fast pocket water, try the high-sticking or Czech method. A wet-fly swing will often work when fish are taking emergers just below or in the surface film.

Mayfly Burrowers

Compared with other mayflies, burrowers are giants. Probably 90 percent of mayfly species can be matched with hooks size 12 or smaller. But with the burrowers, hooks in sizes 10, 8, and occasionally even 6 are needed to match mature nymphs and their winged stages. Something this large and juicy needs to find a way to hide from hungry predators like trout, which may explain why the nymphs evolved the ability to burrow under the stream bottom substrate, where even the most aggressive trout can't find them. Nymphs of some species remain in their underground tunnels two or three years before they reach full size, coming out only at night to feed on decaying organic matter on the bottom, known as detritus.

The burrower group of mayflies is less complex than the others, consisting of just three families, four genera, and half a dozen species. Most species are widespread across North America but become abundant only where stream conditions are just right.

Recognizing burrower nymphs is simple. To burrow into the stream bottom, they all have unique tusklike mandibles, broad front legs designed for digging, and large, tapered, feathery gills that undulate in waves along the abdomen. All burrowers are similar in shape and behavior and can be grouped together for discussion of habitat, behavior, patterns, and fishing methods.

The water that is home to big burrowing mayflies is also home to big trout.

Hexagenias, Drakes, and Others

Families: Ephemeridae, Polymitarcyidae, Potamanthidae
Major genera:

  Hexagenia (hex, big yellow may, Michigan caddis)
  Ephemera (brown drake, yellow drake, eastern green drake)
  Anthopotamus (golden drake)
  Ephoron (whitefly, white drake)

Ephemera guttulata nymph. THOMAS AMES

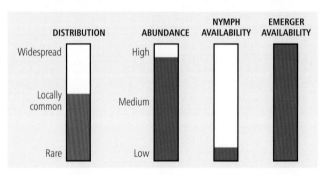

General Information. Burrowers are abundant only in the right substrate, so first you need to find out if they even exist where you are fishing. Ask at local fly shops about their hatches or take samples with a net in likely looking habitat. Because the nymphs often take several years to mature, they should be present in streams year-round. Sample areas with a substrate of soft mud or fine gravel mixed with sand and silt. This habitat occurs only where the current is slow or nonexistent.

The burrower species *Hexagenia limbata* and *Ephemera simulans* have the widest distribution, occurring in streams and lakes from coast to coast. The other main species of burrowers—*Ephemera guttulata, Anthopotamus distinctus,* and *Ephoron leukon*—are important only in midwestern and eastern streams. Burrower populations overall are more common and abundant in the East and Midwest, where there are more low-gradient streams with slow currents and muddy bottoms than in the West.

Habitat. Hexagenia limbata nymphs dig U-shaped tunnels into the finest substrate, preferring claylike mud, in large rivers, small streams, or lakes. The bottom must be soft enough for the nymphs to dig into yet hard enough that the tunnels won't collapse after being dug. Species of *Ephemera* and *Ephoron* dig tunnels into a substrate composed of silt, sand, and fine gravel. The *Anthopotamus* nymphs are the least burrowerlike, crawling under and around a mixed substrate of sand and small stones where the current is more moderate than slow.

Stillwater with a bottom of fine sediment provides the right conditions for many burrower nymphs.

Behavior. Burrowers are unusual mayflies in preferring substrates of mud or fine sand and silt. Their gills are the key to their survival in such fine sediment. Burrower nymphs have large, forked gills with a featherlike fringe of fine filaments. This provides a large surface area for extracting oxygen from the water even when oxygen levels get low. By waving their gills rhythmically along their abdomens, they create their own current of water through their tunnels and over the gills. This movement also cleans fine silt and mud off the gills.

Burrower nymphs spend much of their time burrowing or hiding under the substrate and thus provide few opportunities for trout to find and feed on them. They become slightly more available at night, when they leave their tunnels to feed on decaying organic matter on the substrate. Their greatest availability occurs when they are mature and ready to emerge into duns. Like other mayflies, the nymphs swim to the surface, where they hang in the film while the duns wiggle free onto the water's surface. Unlike other mayflies, burrowers are very large, and like drunks with bar snacks in front of them, trout can't stop eating these tasty morsels while they're emerging. Birds of all persuasions also come to feast on the large duns and spinners flapping off the water or flying through the air. To minimize the slaughter, most burrowers emerge at night, when the cover of darkness provides some safety.

Patterns. Big burrower nymphs swim with a lot of wiggle, so nymph patterns with a lot of motion work best. Hinged, two-part wiggle nymphs and strip nymphs are two imitations that move like the naturals.

Extended Body Burrower Nymph (8–6)

Hexagenia Nymph (8–6)

Fishing Tactics. There's nothing subtle about trout feeding during a hatch of one of the big burrowers. The nymphs are eaten in large numbers as they swim up to the surface, so nymph patterns work well in the early stages of a hatch. Given that most hatches occur in slow water, sinking these large nymphs is not a problem. Because hatches occur at or after dark, a strike indicator is of little help. This is fishing by feel, but you won't be guessing when a big trout slams your fly. The basic approach is to cast up and across a stretch of water where bugs are hatching or will be. Let your nymph sink several feet, and then retrieve it to the surface with short strips. The nymphs swim well, but it is easy to strip too fast— from adrenaline if nothing else—so if you aren't having much success, try slowing down your retrieve a little. If you see fish boiling under the surface, get your nymph to rise up in front of them. You'll be using big flies and catching big fish, so use stout tippets, such as 2X, and don't strike too hard. Setting the hook is rarely a problem.

STONEFLIES: Order Plecoptera

The order Plecoptera, the stoneflies, rivals the mayflies in diversity of species found in streams and rivers, with almost six hundred species sprinkled across North America. Like mayflies, stoneflies are primitive insects, with their first known relatives dating back almost 250 million years. Unlike mayflies, stoneflies don't present the same level of complexity for the angler and can be imitated with fewer patterns and tactics. There are several reasons for this. First, nearly all species of stoneflies live in similar habitat—moderate to fast riffles and runs with a substrate of clean gravel and cobble—and require cold, highly oxygenated, unpolluted water to thrive. Their primitive gill structure restricts stoneflies to this narrow range of habitats. In many species, the gills consist of a few slender,

Giant stoneflies (Pteronarcys californica) *mating on streamside vegetation.*

fingerlike filaments attached under the head or at the base of the legs. Other stonefly species lack gills entirely and breathe directly through thin, membranous areas of the exoskeleton. As a result, most stonefly nymphs must live where the water has plenty of oxygen, something riffle areas in cold-water streams have in abundance.

Another factor that simplifies imitating stoneflies is their behavior. Whereas different mayfly species vary widely in how they move underwater and emerge into adults, the species of stonefly nymphs all behave in much the same way. With few exceptions, stonefly nymphs would best be described as crawlers as they move through their riffle habitat. A few species penetrate several inches to several feet beneath the substrate in their early stages of development, living in a region of the stream bottom called the hyporheic zone, but no stoneflies dig tunnels into the substrate.

Once mature and ready to hatch, stonefly nymphs migrate toward shore, where they crawl out of the water onto the bank and up rocks, logs, trees, or bridges. Adult emergence occurs when the nymphs have reached a suitable spot out of the water. This means adults are not directly available to fish during emergence, though nymph availability increases while they are migrating toward shore. Adults also mate on streamside rocks or foliage. They locate each other for mating by drumming their abdomens on branches or leaves of shoreline vegetation. Males drum one pattern, which is answered by a receptive female with a different pattern. To avoid confusion, each species uses its own drum patterns. This drumming is not heard but is felt by the adults as vibrations through the vegetation. After mating, the females fly back to the water to lay their eggs. This offers fish their best opportunity to see and feed on adult stoneflies.

To help understand pattern selection for stoneflies, the order can be divided into five distinct groups based on size and color: little brown stones, little green stones, little yellow stones, golden stones, and giant stones. The fly patterns, habitat, behavior, and fishing tactics for each of these groups are described below. There is considerable repetition in the information for these five groups because of overlap in shape, behavior, and habitat among the species. By tying just a few pattern styles in a range of colors and sizes, you can effectively imitate all the stoneflies.

Little Brown Stones

Major families: Nemouridae, Leuctriidae, Capniidae,
   Taeniopterygidae
Major genera: *Amphinemura, Nemoura, Zapada,
   Malenka, Leuctra, Allocapnia, Capnia, Mesocapnia,
   Taeniopteryx, Taenionema*

*Nemoura sp., one of the common members of the little
brown stonefly group in the family Nemouridae.* DAVE HUGHES

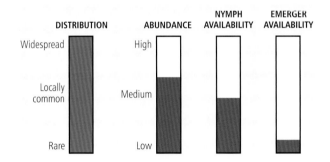

General Information. The little brown stones are the most
diverse of the five groups of stoneflies, with four major
families, thirty-five genera, and more than three hundred
species. Species of all four families are widely represented
across North America, though most occur in moderate
abundance and only rarely seem to be the target of selective feeding. Though this group is highly diverse, nymphs
and adults of nearly all species range from a uniform light
brown to almost black and vary from size 18 to 14.
Nymphs tend to be slender and rather delicate looking.
Some species are referred to as needle flies because of
their slender shape.

   Though some adults can be found emerging year-
round, the greatest activity tends to occur in the late winter and early spring. Many species of the family Capniidae
have the unique habit of emerging into adults during the
coldest period of the year, December through March,
which gave them their other common name of winter
stoneflies. Species that frequently produce fishable popu-

lations include *Zapada cinctipes* (little sepia stonefly) and
Malenka californica (little western stonefly) in western
streams and *Strophopteryx fasciata* (little red stonefly or
February red) in eastern streams.

Habitat. Given the wide variety of species in this group, it
should be no surprise that little brown stones can be
found in a range of stream types. Nymphs are equally
common in small creeks to large rivers and tailwater
rivers to spring creeks. Most species seek out areas with
moderate current flow where organic debris, such as piles
of decaying leaves, has accumulated. This provides both
cover and protection from predators and the nymphs'
primary food source. In cold mountain streams, nymphs
are frequently found in riffles with substrate of small to
moderate-size gravel.

*Many little brown stonefly species emerge when snow still
covers the landscape.*

Behavior. Most little brown stone nymphs feed on decaying leaves and other organic debris. This allows them to
hide and generally stay out of the water column where
feeding trout might see them. Mature nymphs migrate to
the edges of stream banks before crawling out to emerge
in typical stonefly fashion. Since many species emerge
in the winter and early spring, this is the time of their
highest availability and thus the best time to imitate
nymphs and adults. It is not uncommon to see adults
crawling over several feet of snow along streams on
bright, sunny winter days. These adults are often wing-
less, giving them the odd appearance of black ants crawling around on snow.

Patterns. Just about any simple small brown nymph pattern tied slender and in the right size will provide an adequate imitation. Since these nymph patterns need to be
kept slender, adding weight to the body of fly usually
makes their silhouette too plump. Add a beadhead or split
shot to your leader to get these fly patterns to the bottom.

Little Brown Stone Nymph (16–12)

Mathew's Amber Stone Nymph (16–12)

Pheasant Tail Soft-Hackle (16–12)

Fishing Tactics. Most situations where I have found little brown stone nymph patterns useful have been in the late winter or early spring on small to medium-size streams. Look for adults along the bank. If you see them in good number, choose a nymph pattern about the same size, and fish it below gentle runs or riffles where good trout habitat occurs. Fish will be used to seeing nymphs along the bottom close to shore, so cover water near the bank before fishing farther out in the channel. Basic tactics like the shot and indicator method are usually all that's needed.

Little Green Stones

Family: Chloroperlidae
Major genera: *Alloperla, Sweltsa, Suwallia*

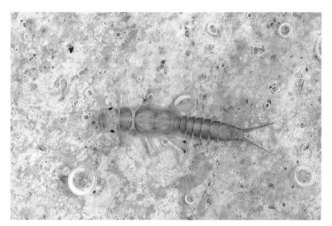

Little green stone nymph (Chloroperlidae). DAVE HUGHES

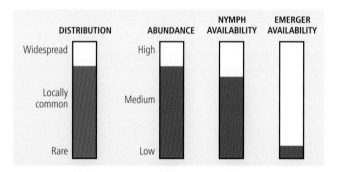

General Information. The little green stones all fall into a single family, Chloroperlidae, with thirteen genera and almost eighty species in North America. Little green stones are common inhabitants of most trout streams, but their abundance and availability vary widely. As a result, their importance also varies. In streams where they are abundant, nymph patterns are most effective just before adult emergence, which begins in late spring and lasts through mid-summer, generally June through August.

Mature nymphs are small to moderate in size, 3/8 to 5/8 inch long, and tend to be quite plain in appearance. The common name refers to the adults, which typically have bright green bodies, though some have yellow bodies. The nymphs of a few species have green bodies, but most are light brown. Most important species to fly fishers include the abundant *Sweltsa coloradensis* (little olive stonefly) in western trout streams and *Alloperla imbecilla* (little green stonefly) in eastern streams.

Habitat. Little green stones inhabit cold streams and rivers with clean gravel bottoms. Young nymphs spend their time around rocks and cobble in riffle areas. As they mature, they often move to less rapid water where organic material such as leaves and twigs has accumulated. Nymphs migrate to shoreline areas and crawl out of the water to emerge into adults.

Choppy riffles and the slick water downstream provide good habitat for little green stoneflies.

Behavior. Nymphs of little green stones are primarily predators, feeding on small midge larvae. Though not rapid crawlers, the nymphs do move actively searching for prey and get into the stream drift. When nymphs are abundant, they can be numerous enough in the drift to be targeted by feeding trout. Annual nymphal migrations toward shore before emergence increase their abundance in the drift. Adult activity is greatest in the late afternoon and evening on pleasant summer days. Swarms of females form over riffle areas and drop to the water's surface to lay their eggs. After doing so, many females sink underwater, where they are eaten by trout.

Patterns. A small brown nymph pattern in the right size is usually effective for imitating little green stone nymphs. Though most species have brown nymphs, a few are green, so it is useful to collect some naturals from the stream you are fishing to determine what color your patterns should be. I like something with soft fibers for legs that will wiggle in the water and add some life to the pattern.

Light Tan Beadhead Hare's Ear (16–12)

Olive Flymph (16–12)

Fishing Tactics. Early-summer mornings and evenings are prime times to use nymph patterns for this group of stoneflies. Fish riffle tailouts and areas near shore with moderate currents that also have good water for holding fish. Though nymphs drift, they are not good swimmers, and patterns should be fished dead drift near the bottom. An upstream-and-across presentation with the shot and indicator method is usually effective.

Little Yellow Stones

Families: Perlodidae, Peltoperlidae

Major genera: *Isoperla, Isogenoides, Skwala, Megarcys, Peltoperla*

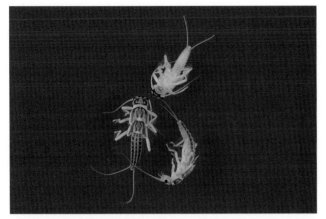

Isoperla *nymphs.* DAVE HUGHES

Skwala *nymph.* DAVE HUGHES

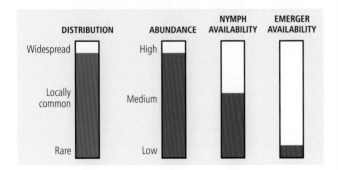

General Information. Perlodidae is by far the more important of the two families in this group of stoneflies, with more than a hundred species found in North America. Peltoperlidae has only eighteen species on the continent, and they tend to be sporadically distributed though occasionally abundant. The genus *Isoperla* contains almost sixty species and provides the bulk of the hatches important to anglers. *I. bilineata* produces some of the

best hatches in eastern streams, and *I. mormona* in western streams.

Little yellow stones come in two distinct size categories. *Isogenoides, Skwala,* and *Megarcys* species are moderately large, at 1 to 1 1/4 inches long, excluding tails. *Isoperla* and *Peltoperla* species are small, at 3/8 to 5/8 inch. The large species emerge primarily in the spring and early summer; the smaller ones are most active as adults in the middle of summer. Nearly all nymphs have yellowish bodies, and many have dramatic dark brown or black markings on the head, thorax, and abdomen. Adults range in color from bright yellow to dark orange.

Habitat. Most little yellow stones live in swift-water riffles with rocky substrate typical of many stoneflies. Species of Peltoperlidae are most abundant where aquatic moss covers the surface of rocks in moderately fast riffles and runs. Some species prefer small streams and creeks, and others large rivers. Many species have no gills or very small ones, so no matter what size streams they prefer, good populations occur only in cold water with high oxygen levels. Like other stonefly nymphs, they migrate to shore before crawling out to emerge into adults.

Moderate to fast riffles with a gravel and cobble bottom provide the right conditions for little yellow stone nymphs and attract females returning to lay their eggs.

Behavior. Little yellow stone nymphs are active predators, searching out smaller mayflies, caddisflies, and midges to dine on. This active lifestyle coupled with the fast-water habitat means nymphs often end up in stream drift, where they become available to fish. Nymph patterns can be effective when the nymphs are abundant. The number of nymphs in the drift also increases when mature nymphs migrate to stream banks prior to adult emergence. Adult *Isoperla* species are the most obvious in this group, as the females gather in large swarms over riffles on warm summer evenings to lay eggs on the water's surface. Like the little green stones, females drop to the water's surface to release their eggs. Trout take the egg-laying females off the surface, but many females also sink underwater after laying their eggs, providing fish subsurface food as well.

Patterns. Because of the two different size categories of little yellow stones, you may need patterns as large as size 8 or as small as size 16. Nymphs of most species live on the bottom in relatively swift water, so your patterns should be weighted to help them sink. Even with additional weight on the hook, you often need to add split shot to the leader to get your fly to the bottom.

Mercer's Gold Dust (16–10)

Beadhead Red Squirrel Nymph (16–10)

Smurf Stone (16–10)

Partridge and Yellow Soft-Hackle (16–10)

Fishing Tactics. Little yellow stone nymph patterns should be fished dead drift along the bottom in riffles and runs and near banks where nymphs have migrated for emergence. The shot and indicator method works in smaller streams with moderate current speeds and larger streams with faster, deeper water, but depending on the type of water you are fishing, the high-sticking, Czech, or Brooks method may be more effective.

Golden Stones

Family: Perlidae

Major genera: *Calineuria, Hesperoperla, Agnetina, Perlesta, Acroneuria, Attaneuria*

Calineuria californica *nymph.* DAVE HUGHES

Recently molted golden stone nymph (Hesperoperla pacifica). DAVE HUGHES

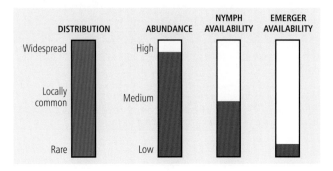

General Information. Golden stones all fall into a single family, Perlidae, with fifteen genera and more than sixty species widely distributed across North America. Different common names have been used for various species, depending on the part of the country you live in. Though I'm using golden stone as a general common name for the group, the term applies more specifically to the two dominant western species, *Calineuria californica* and *Hesperoperla pacifica.* The common names of eastern species include the great brown stonefly *(Acroneuria lycorias),* eastern stonefly creeper *(Agnetina capitata),* and yellow-legged stonefly *(Attaneuria ruralis).*

Mature golden stone nymphs reach lengths well over an inch long, excluding their tails. To reach this size, nymphs often require two and sometimes three years of growth. This means that multiple size classes of nymphs can be found in streams throughout the year. All nymphs in the family Perlidae have bushy clumps of gills attached at the base of each leg, and a few species have similar clumps between the two tails. The color of golden stone nymphs varies widely among the species. Some are dark brown with light ribbing, others yellowish brown with dark markings on the head and thorax, and still others a uniform light brown. Most common names refer to the coloration of the adults, which also varies among species.

Habitat. These large stoneflies prefer fast water in riffles with a substrate of large cobble and boulders. Streams of all sizes may have good populations as long as riffles are present and the water is cold and unpolluted. After several years in fast riffle areas, mature nymphs migrate to quieter water near shore just before crawling out for emergence. After adults emerge, the large, empty exoskeletons of the nymphs remain attached to trees, rocks, and bridge abutments for months along many streams, providing a good reminder that younger nymphs still crawl along the bottom.

Fast riffles and the bank water nearby provide excellent habitat for many stoneflies, including golden stones.

Behavior. Nymphs of golden stones are among the largest and most aggressive insect predators found in streams, rivaled only by the fierce hellgrammite larvae. These big nymphs will routinely eat smaller nymphs in trays of insects collected for streamside fishing classes. It takes less than a minute for a golden stone nymph to completely consume a ¹/₂-inch-long mayfly or caddisfly larva. Such predatory behavior means these big nymphs actively hunt their prey in the riffles where they live. Because of their large size, however, the nymphs do not drift in current as frequently or as far as the smaller stonefly nymphs of the other groups.

The greatest exposure of these big nymphs to trout occurs when they migrate to shore before adult emergence. Depending on a stream's location and elevation, emergence may begin as early as May or as late as August. Nymphal migration activity puts more nymphs into the drift and gets trout on the lookout for a big, easy meal. Several days after emerging, adults mate on streamside foliage, and a few days later, females fly out over the riffles to lay their eggs. When adults are present in large numbers, trout often feed with a reckless attitude, and some of the biggest trout in a stream are easily fooled with large dry flies plopped onto the surface.

Patterns. Many tiers take imitation to new levels when creating patterns for these large, colorful stonefly nymphs. Such realistic patterns are works of art in their own right,

Mercer's Brown Stone (12–6)

John's Beadhead Golden Stone (12–6)

but they do not catch more fish. In fact, my preference is for less imitative patterns that provide more movement underwater. Charlie Brooks's Montana Stone pattern does an excellent job of this and has been one of my favorite stonefly nymph patterns for many years. Because the nymphs of these species don't all mature at the same time, younger, smaller nymphs remain available year-round. To imitate these smaller nymphs effectively, use smaller patterns in sizes 12 and 10. I often find these smaller patterns more effective than large size 8 and 6 flies tied to match the size of mature nymphs.

Beadhead Brook's Stone (12–6)

Smurf Stone (12–6)

Fishing Tactics. A large nymph fished just off the bottom in fast water is the name of the game when imitating these large stoneflies. The Brooks method was developed just for this purpose and works great in runs in large rivers with fast water over three feet deep. In riffles in small to medium streams or when fishing quieter water along the banks, the shot and indicator approach is a good method to use. If you are working up a riffle or run with good pocket water, try the high-sticking or Czech method.

Giant Stones

Family: Pteronarcidae
Major genera: *Pteronarcys, Pteronarcella*

Pteronarcys californica *nymph.* DAVE HUGHES

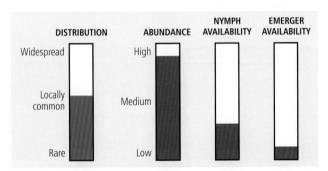

General Information. Several species of the family Pteronarcidae are the largest stoneflies found in North America, with mature nymphs reaching more than two inches long, excluding tails. Giant stone nymphs take three or four years to grow to this impressive size. This is not a diverse group, with just two genera and ten species occurring across the continent. Though giant stones live in streams from coast to coast, their distribution is spotty. Some streams harbor very large populations, while other streams have none. Because of their size, however, it is easy to find them when they are present. Perhaps the most famous of the giant stones is the western species *Pteronarcys californica,* commonly called the salmon fly because the adult's reddish underbelly resembles the color of spawning salmon. The most common species in eastern and midwestern streams is *P. dorsata,* often called the giant black stonefly.

One might assume that such large stoneflies are predaceous like the golden stones, but giant stones feed primarily on detritus, decaying plant matter and wood debris. This feeding behavior requires little movement, and for the most part these big nymphs remain hidden and avoid hungry trout.

Giant stone nymphs can be easily recognized by their near uniform dark brown to black color, very short stout tails, and clumps of bushy filamentous gills lined up along the underside of the thorax and first two or three abdominal segments. Pteronarcid nymphs are one of the only stoneflies in North America with gills anywhere on the abdomen.

Habitat. Giant stones use the same fast-water riffle habitat preferred by golden stones and the smaller little yellow stones. Riffles with large cobble and boulders that trap organic debris provide the perfect conditions for these detritus-feeding nymphs. Most of the best-known hatches occur on large western rivers, such as Madison in Montana, Gunnison in Colorado, and Deschutes in Oregon. These streams all have extensive riffle habitat with large rocky substrate. As with all other stoneflies, mature nymphs migrate from their fast-water homes to shoreline areas, where they crawl out on rocks or trees above the water for adult emergence.

Behavior. Giant stoneflies are a good example of how size alone does not determine importance to fish and anglers. Though these are some of the biggest insects found in

Drifting a nymph pattern of a giant stonefly off the bottom in heavy riffles, the species' preferred habitat, can produce some exciting results.

North American streams, they are often of minor importance as food for trout. Both their size and feeding behavior limit their exposure and likelihood of drifting in the current, and many trout streams have small populations of these large stoneflies. In streams with large populations, however, fishing a nymph pattern during the migration to shore prior to adult emergence can result in excellent fishing.

Adult giant stones mate on streamside foliage like other stonefly adults. A few days after mating, females fly back out over the water and either release clusters of eggs a few feet above the water or drop down to the surface to lay their eggs. In either case, the egg-laying females provide a large meal for hungry trout and are often the focus of dry-fly fishermen when adults are abundant. Many western streams have both salmon flies and golden stones present, and adult emergence of the two groups often overlaps. When this happens, trout almost always prefer golden stone over salmon fly adults. My hunch is that golden stone adults taste better, but I haven't confirmed this yet!

Patterns. The same pattern styles used for golden stone nymphs work for giant stonefly nymphs; you just need to modify their size and color appropriately. Because of the heavy fast water in which these flies are typically fished, they should be weighted with plenty of lead wire to help them sink. Also like the golden stones, the giant stone nymphs take several years to mature, so the majority of nymphs in the stream throughout most of the year (except for the two- or three-week period just before emergence) are much smaller than the large, mature nymphs found in late spring and early summer. I find that smaller patterns, such as sizes 12 and 10, usually take more fish than the big patterns tied to imitate mature nymphs.

Fishing Tactics. The tactics for fishing giant stones are the same as those used for golden stones. Getting your nymph

Large stoneflies come in many sizes. Imitating the younger, smaller nymphs is often most effective. DAVE HUGHES

Brook's Stone (12–4)

Black Stone (12–4)

Smurf Stone (12–4)

pattern to the bottom in fast water is the primary objective, so the best method to use depends on how deep and fast the water is where you are fishing. The Brooks method is best for fishing the deepest and fastest runs in large rivers. In shallower or slower water, the shot and indicator method is my first choice. When fishing pocket water, the high-sticking and Czech methods work well. However, don't get fixated on these large stoneflies when you find them in the stream you are fishing. Even when giant stoneflies are abundant, they are not usually the dominant nymph being eaten by trout, and smaller mayfly or caddisfly nymph patterns are generally more effective.

CADDISFLIES: Order Trichoptera

The order Trichoptera, the caddisflies, is incredibly diverse, with almost 1,400 species, 147 genera, and 22 families known in North America. Overall, there are more species of caddisflies than all the mayflies and stoneflies put together. Caddisflies occur across the whole spectrum of freshwater habitat found in streams, rivers, lakes, and ponds. Species' tolerance to different water-quality conditions also varies widely. Some species of caddisflies, like stoneflies, require cold, highly oxygenated water found in riffle areas of clean, undisturbed streams. Others thrive where the water is warm, even thermally heated, and oxygen levels are low from either natural causes or human activity and pollution. This means that as a fly fisher, you will encounter caddisflies, often in abundance, in just about any water you fish.

Caddisflies undergo complete metamorphosis and thus have four different stages in their life cycle: egg, larva, pupa, and adult. For most species, it takes a year to complete all four stages (one generation), but some species complete two or three generations in a single year, and others take two or three years per generation. Most of their life cycle is spent as larvae feeding along the bottom of streams or lakes. Larval feeding behavior and general availability to trout vary widely among species. Most caddisfly larvae exhibit the unique behavior of building tube-like cases out of a wide range of materials, such as sand, gravel, twigs, bark, leaves, or pine needles, which serve as cozy homes and provide protection from predators. Different species use different types of materials and build specific types of cases. Though cases are one of the most obvious characteristics of caddisfly larvae, not all species build them.

Once fully grown, larvae molt into the pupal stage. Pupation occurs inside the larval cases hidden under rocks and debris on stream or lake bottoms. Species that do not build cases as larvae usually construct rough caselike shelters for pupation. Pupae require one to two months before they are mature and ready to make their final transition into adults. Then they leave their underwater hideouts and swim to the water's surface, where adult emergence takes place. Though most pupae can swim well, trout have no trouble catching them during their ascent, and pupal patterns can be very effective and important to use during caddis hatches. Adults mate on streamside foliage. After several days to weeks, females return to the water to lay their eggs. The females of many species dive underwater and swim to the bottom to deposit their eggs. This puts

Cases built by caddis larvae provide them with protection and a distinctive appearance. DAVE HUGHES

them once more right in front of hungry trout, which readily take advantage of the situation.

Because of their behavior, larvae, pupae, and adults all can be the focus of selective feeding by trout. And because larvae, pupae, and even some adults are available to trout underwater, all three stages can be important to imitate with nymphs and wet flies fished anywhere from close to the bottom to just under the surface.

All of this adds up to a complex order with a wide range of species that live in various water types with a number of behaviors that call for imitation with different patterns and tactics. This complexity can be simplified by breaking the order into six groups based on larval size and behavior: green rock worms, net-spinning caddis, lesser net-spinning caddis, saddle-case caddis, American Grannom, and cased caddis. By becoming familiar with these six different groups and knowing where and how they live, you will be able to select effective patterns and tactics for this large and terribly important order.

Because this is such a large, diverse order, you will occasionally run into other caddisflies during your fishing that this book does not specifically cover. One such group is the family Hydroptilidae, the microcaddis. Though these insects are widespread and often abundant, they are usually too small to imitate. Most species I have collected would require a size 28 or smaller fly pattern. Also, only caddis important in streams and rivers are included here. Lakes have another set of caddisfly species with their own interesting behaviors, hatch periods, and patterns to match them.

Green Rock Worms

Family: Rhyacophilidae
Major genus: *Rhyacophila*

*Green rock worm larva (*Rhyacophila *sp.).* DAVE HUGHES

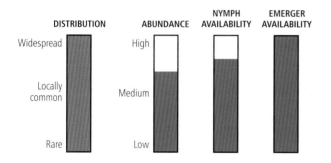

General Information. Green rock worms all belong to a single family, Rhyacophilidae. There is only one important genus, *Rhyacophila,* which contains about 126 species in North American streams. As a result, green rock worms occur in most streams across the continent. Besides being widely distributed, they also occur in abundance in many of the streams they live in. When abundant, these larvae frequently end up on the menu of feeding trout. Unlike most caddisfly larvae, green rock worm larvae built no cases and thus are often called free-living caddis. Being caseless or free-living, green rock worm larvae are more vulnerable and available to feeding trout than most cased caddis larvae.

Given the wide diversity of species, not all green rock worm larvae are green. Some are dark olive or even dirty brown. The majority, however, come in various shades of green, some almost chartreuse. Mature larvae range in size from $1/2$ to $3/4$ inch long. When ready to pupate, larvae crawl into cracks between large rocks and cover themselves with sand and fine gravel. Hidden in these small gravel shelters, pupae take four to six weeks to develop. When fully developed, the pupae cut out of their shelters and swim to the water's surface, where the adults quickly escape the pupal exoskeletons and fly away. Like the larvae, most pupae are some shade of green. Adults have olive to brown bodies and mottled gray wings.

Developing green rock worm pupa inside pupal cell.

Habitat. Green rock worms live in swift, bouncy riffles, particularly liking those with medium to large rocks and cobble on the bottom. The rocks provide plenty of places to hide from the full force of the current and good cracks and crevices in which to pupate when they are ready. Green rock worms use habitat very similar to that used by most stonefly nymphs, and it is common when collecting to find both in the same samples.

Cool mountain streams with cobble-bottomed riffles are home to a variety of green rock worm species.

Behavior. Caddis larvae are not noted for their swimming ability, and green rock worms are no exception. Even though they live in swift-water habitat, once they get into the current, they drift more or less helplessly until they can grab another rock or stone on the bottom. Green rock worms also occur commonly in behavioral drift in the early morning and evening. As a result, nymph patterns imitating the green rock worm larvae often produce well when fished dead drift just off the stream bottom.

Pupae are more active in the water than the larvae. They use their hind legs like oars for swimming to the surface to emerge, and they release small bubbles of gas under the exoskeleton to help it quickly split open when they reach the water's surface. Employing their legs for propulsion and gas bubbles for lift, pupae quickly reach the surface with a quick, erratic swimming action. Still, because they live in fast riffles, the pupae drift some distance downstream and provide trout good opportunities to feed on them.

Adult green rock worms mate on streamside foliage. When females return to lay their eggs, they dive or crawl underwater until they reach the stream bottom, where they deposit strings of eggs. Females have specially designed hind legs for swimming. Once their eggs have been deposited, they release their hold on the bottom and drift slowly back toward the surface. These egg-laying adults spend more time drifting in the current than do emerging pupae, so fish often target the submerged females.

With so many different species, it is hard to predict just when major hatches of green rock worms will occur. In most streams, there are good hatches in the spring and fall, March through May and September through October.

Patterns. To cover the different underwater stages available to trout, you need good nymph, pupa, and submerged adult patterns. Nymph patterns are simple larval

Green Rock Worm (14–10)

Morrish's Supper Pupa (14–10)

Beadhead Krystal Flash Caddis (14–10)

LaFontaine Deep Sparkle Pupa (14–10)

Beadhead Green Rock Worm (14–10)

Translucent Diving Caddis (14–10)

imitations that should be weighted to help sink them to the bottom in fast riffles. For pupae and submerged adults, I prefer patterns tied with some loose, soft materials to help give them more lifelike action in the water.

Fishing Tactics. The best approach depends on the life stage you are imitating. Since the larvae don't swim but drift close to the bottom, the shot and indicator or high-sticking method will usually do the trick. During a hatch, when the pupae are rising to the surface, the Leisenring lift is perfect. Try to position yourself so you get your pupa imitation rising up right in front of the feeding trout. Trout taking pupae often make vigorous, splashy rises. When the adults are laying eggs, try a simple wet-fly swing. It might be helpful to add split shot to your leader twelve to eighteen inches from the fly to help sink it a foot or two below the surface. Since females do not swim quickly to the surface, you won't need to add the same rising action to your fly as you do for pupae. Given the fast-water habitat green rock worms prefer, focus on riffles when fishing their imitations. Look for trout actively feeding or areas with good structure for holding trout.

Clear water, clear skies, and a gorgeous setting: Sometimes it's easy to forget to fish.

Net-Spinning Caddis
Family: Hydropsychidae
Major genera: *Hydropsyche, Cheumatopsyche*

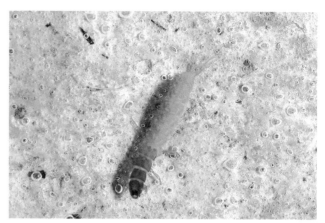

Net-spinning caddis larva (Cheumatopsyche *sp.*).

DAVE HUGHES

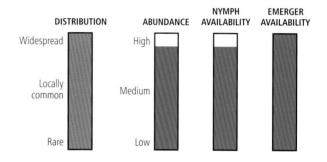

General Information. In streams and rivers, the net-spinning caddis, family Hydropsychidae, may be the most important caddisfly of all. This family is highly diverse and widespread, with more than 140 species in twelve genera occurring in all types of streams throughout North America. They are often very abundant, and larvae, pupae, and adults are routinely available to feeding trout. Species from two genera produce most of the major caddis hatches in trout streams across the country: *Hydropsyche* (sometimes called spotted sedges) and *Cheumatopsyche* (sometimes called little olive sedges). If there is one group of caddisflies you should know and be prepared to imitate, it is the net-spinning caddis.

Net-spinning caddis larvae look surprisingly similar to green rock worm larvae. They overlap in both size and color, with net spinners ranging from $1/4$ to $3/4$ inch long and from bright green to dark brown. They also overlap in shape and habitat. With all these similarities, how can you tell them apart? In the larval stage, two simple features help distinguish net-spinning caddis from green rock worms. First, look at the upper surface of the thoracic segments. In net-spinning caddis larvae, all three of these segments have hard, dark brown plates, but in green rock worm larvae, only the first segment right behind the head is hard and dark brown. Second, all net-spinning caddis larvae have a row of bushy filamentous gills running down the underside of the abdomen. Green rock worm larvae either lack gills or have ones that are in patches of filaments along the sides of the abdomen, never in a row under the abdomen. Recognizing pupae or adults between the two groups is more difficult but generally not necessary. As long as you know the size and color of the pupa or adult you are trying to imitate, you can select an effective pattern.

Gills along the underside of the abdomen is characteristic of a net-spinning caddis larva. DAVE HUGHES

Habitat. Net-spinning caddis, like green rock worms, prefer to live in riffles with a rocky substrate. Given the diversity of species, however, net-spinning larvae can be found in a wide range of stream conditions. Some prefer areas with finer substrate, such as sand and small gravel, and moderate currents. Others like submerged logs and snags. But wherever there are moderate to fast riffle areas with a cobble and boulder substrate, there will likely be good numbers of net-spinning caddis larvae. The numbers of net-spinning caddis larvae can be particularly high in tailwater streams below dams. That's because the zooplankton and phytoplankton that grow in reservoirs get washed downstream, where they provide an excellent food source for net-spinning larvae.

Pupation occurs in the same habitat used by the larvae. After four to six weeks, the pupae are mature and make their ascent to the surface for emergence. After emerging, adults fly to streamside vegetation, where they wait a few days before mating.

Choppy riffles hold thousands of net-spinning caddis larvae and can be excellent places to fish their larva and pupa patterns.

*Net-spinning caddis pupa (*Hydropsyche *sp.).* DAVE HUGHES

Behavior. Their name should give you some clue about the behavior of the net-spinning caddis. The larvae construct nets out of silk threads, much like the webs made by spiders. The nets vary in size from roughly the diameter of a dime up to a quarter. How the nets are constructed and where they are placed differs among species. Most place their nets on the side or upper surface of a large cobblestone or boulder, where the current is relatively fast. The net is positioned so the current flows directly into it and effectively strains drifting food items out of the water. The larva often attaches its net to a rough shelter of small twigs or gravel. It then waits inside the shelter until enough food has been trapped in the net to make it worth the effort to crawl out and eat it.

The mesh size of the nets varies with the type of stream the larvae live in. Nets in small headwater streams have a large mesh, whereas those far downstream in the watersheds of large rivers have a fine mesh. This makes sense when you consider that the food drifting in headwater areas has not been broken down into small pieces and is therefore relatively large and coarse, best strained

Net-spinning caddis larvae attach their retreats and nets to the sides of submerged rocks.

Larval overcrowding results in frequent drifting of net-spinning caddis larvae.

from the current by a large-meshed net. By the time drifting food items end up miles and miles downstream, they have been ground or broken up into very fine particles, which requires a fine-meshed net to filter from the water.

Net-spinning caddis larvae often suffer from overcrowding. This occurs when so many nets get built on the same rock that some nets block the current to others. The larvae with nets blocked by an upstream net get little or no food, so they must leave the area and find a less crowded rock. The easiest way to do this is to simply let go of the rock and drift downstream to a different one. To minimize overcrowding and prevent intrusion by other larvae, net-spinning larvae of the genus *Hydropsyche* use a unique territorial behavior. Under the head is a series of striations, which are drawn across a ridge on each femur of the front legs to produce a chirping sound. This is detectable to humans only with a microphone. So next time you are standing in a riffle fishing, keep in mind that thousands of net-spinning caddis larvae are chirping beneath the water. Overcrowding still occurs, however, and the larvae are abun-

dant in stream drift as a result and regularly end up on the food tray of feeding trout.

The pupal and adult stages of net-spinning caddis are also available to feeding trout. Pupae become available when they swim up to the surface during adult emergence. Most adult hatches of this group occur in the summer months, from June through August. Adults get eaten on the surface during a hatch, but more important is when females return in the evening to lay their eggs. Like the green rock worm females, net-spinning caddis females dive underwater and swim to the bottom. After they have deposited their eggs, the females let go and drift slowly back up to the surface. Such behavior offers trout plenty of feeding opportunities.

Patterns. The same pattern styles used to imitate green rock worms can be used for net-spinning caddis. Since size and color of the two groups overlap, at times the exact same patterns can be used for both groups. This is not always the case, however, so take a quick look at the naturals in the stream to confirm what size and color pattern you should use.

Barr's Gold-Bead Net-Spinning Caddis in tan (top) *and green* (bottom) *(16–12)*

Net-Spinning Caddis (16–12)

08.20 Zug Bug (16–12)

LaFontaine Emergent Sparkle Pupa (16–12)

Tan CDC Flymph (16–12)

CDC Beadhead Pheasant Tail Emerger (16–12)

Fishing Tactics. The fishing methods for net-spinning caddis and green rock worms also overlap. Larvae primarily live and drift along the bottom in riffle areas, so the shot and indicator and high-sticking methods work well when using nymph patterns. During a hatch, pupal behavior is imitated well with a Leisenring lift. When adult females are laying their eggs underwater, a wet-fly swing is usually effective.

Lesser Net-Spinning Caddis

Major families: Philopotamidae, Psychomyiidae,
  Polycentropodidae
Major genera: *Chimarra, Wormaldia, Psychomyia,
  Polycentropus, Nyctiophylax, Lype*

*Lesser net-spinning caddis larva (Philopotamidae:
Wormaldia sp.).* DAVE HUGHES

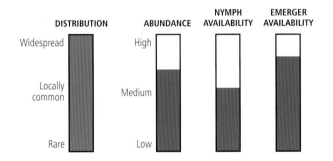

General Information. The name lesser net-spinning caddis is used because these caddis are smaller and less obvious than the Hydropsychidae, not because this group is less diverse or less common. The group includes three widely distributed families, four to six common and important genera, and in total more than 130 species.

These species also build nets to strain food out of the current, but their nets are small silk funnels or long, slender bags attached to rocks or debris on the stream bottom, rather than the spinnaker-shaped, spiderweblike nets constructed by species of Hydropsychidae. The small nets often get covered with silt and fine detritus and can easily go unnoticed even when abundant. I usually spot the slender, 1/4- to 1/2-inch-long, cream to yellow larvae crawling inchworm fashion over the surfaces of stones I have lifted out of the water. When abundant, dozens of larvae can be seen crawling over one softball-size rock.

Overall, this group is more abundant and important in midwestern and eastern trout streams than in western ones. Some of the most important species include

Nyctiophylax moestus (dinky light summer sedge) and *Polycentropus cinereus* (brown checkered summer sedge) in the family Polycentropodidae; *Lype diversa* (dark eastern woodland sedge) and *Psychomyia flavida* (dinky purple-breasted sedge) in the family Psychomyiidae; and *Chimarra aterrima* (little black sedge) in the family Philopotamidae. Most species can be matched with small patterns from size 16 to 22. The primary hatches occur from April through August, depending on the species and habitat.

Habitat. The lesser net-spinning caddis prefer much slower-flowing water than other net spinners. Larvae usually position their nets on the undersides of rocks or wood debris in gently flowing flats or slower currents along streamside banks. A few species are as common along the wave-washed shorelines of lakes as they are in streams. Some species thrive only in cold, well-oxygenated small mountain streams, but others do best in relatively warm water and can be extremely abundant in large, slow-flowing valley rivers. Pupation occurs inside the larval nets.

Gentle runs and flats provide the right conditions for lesser net-spinning caddis larvae.

Behavior. Because the larvae inhabit relatively slow water, they are not as common in stream drift as species that live in fast riffle areas. Still, larvae do drift, and if they appear to be the dominant insect in samples collected from your stream, don't hesitate to imitate them with small nymph patterns. Their greatest availability, however, generally occurs during hatches, when the pupae swim to the surface for emergence, and when the females return to the water to lay their eggs. The females of some species dive underwater and swim to the bottom to deposit eggs; others drift quietly on the surface. In both cases, the females are readily available to feeding trout.

Patterns. Small versions of common pattern styles for caddis larvae, pupae, and diving adults work for this group of caddis. Colors vary, but in most cases the larvae are tan to yellow, and pupae and adults tend to range from light brown to almost black.

Beadhead Caddis Larva (20–14)

Cream CDC Flymph (20–14)

Fishing Tactics. When imitating these little caddisflies, you will be using small patterns and most likely fishing in smooth, slow-flowing sections of streams, so lightweight lines and rods that allow more delicate presentations will

Mercer's Z-wing Caddis (20–14)

Silvey's Prime Pupa Tan (20–14)

be helpful. For nymphing, you don't need heavy flies or a lot of weight on your leader, but you still need to get your fly to the right depth without making a lot of disturbance on the surface. The hinged-leader method is well suited for these situations. When pupae are rising to emerge or females are diving underwater to lay their eggs, you will see fish feeding close to the surface; this is a perfect situation for the Leisenring lift. In clear water where you can spot individual fish feeding, the Skues and Sawyer methods will work.

Saddle-Case Caddis

Family: Glossosomatidae
Major genera: *Glossosoma, Agapetus, Protoptila*

Glossosoma *larva.* DAVE HUGHES

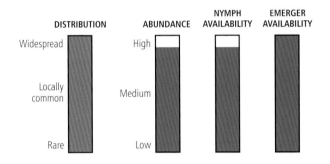

General Information. This group consists of a single family, Glossosomatidae, with six genera, three of which are important in trout streams, and seventy-six species occurring across North America. The saddle-case caddis is named for the distinctive case built by this small caddisfly. Instead of the typical cylindrical case built by most cased caddisflies, this case resembles a dome or turtle shell with a small strap, or saddle, across the underside that allows the larva's head and rear to protrude, though neither is visible from above. This is a primitive design, and Glossosomatidae is considered to have been one of the first families of caddisflies to attempt case building. The adults in this family are often called little tan short-horn caddis.

Saddle-case caddisflies are common and widespread, and they can be extremely abundant. Species of *Agapetus* and *Protoptila* seem to prefer warmer streams than species of *Glossosoma*, which is dominant in higher, colder mountain streams. The other two genera become more abundant as one moves downstream into warmer waters. Species of all three genera can produce excellent hatches, but *Glossosoma* species tend to be the most abundant and important in trout streams. This is a widespread genus, with species occurring across North America.

Most anglers tend to overlook these well-camouflaged caddis, perhaps because of their small size, which typically ranges from 18 to 20, or because they blend in so well with their surroundings. Overlooking them, however, is a mistake. Gary LaFontaine made this clear in his book *Caddisflies* when he wrote, "Not just among caddisflies, but among the entire fauna in many trout rivers the larvae, pupae, and adults of *Glossosoma* create more selective feeding situations than any other organism at certain times of the year."

Glossosoma *cases on rocks.*

Habitat. The larvae of this group are riffle dwellers. Pick up just about any rock from baseball to bowling ball size in a moderate to fast riffle in a cold trout stream, and you are likely to see numerous small, dome-shaped cases of *Glossosoma* attached to the sides and top. Because the cases blend in so well with the surrounding stones, it is easy to pay them little attention. Even if you do notice them, the larvae don't appear to be available to trout, as their cases provide a secure cover. But their behavior makes them much more available than they appear. When larvae have reached full size, they pupate under their cases in the same habitat.

Behavior. The larvae are perfectly suited to their life in riffles. Their cases stick tightly to the bottom, affording protection from the current and predators. Larvae feed by moving slowly over the surfaces of rocks, scraping off the periphyton, the thin layer of diatoms and algae, as they go. Fish would have little opportunity to feed on these larvae if it weren't for one problem: As the larva grows, it periodically gets too large for its case and has to abandon it in order to build a new one. When it crawls free of the old case, the larva gets washed into the drift. The timing of new case building appears to be synchronized such that the majority of larvae leave their old cases at approximately the same time, causing large numbers to enter the drift at once. This creates perfect conditions for trout

Clean gravel in cold mountain streams produces the best populations of saddle-case caddis.

to feed selectively on the small larvae. Gary LaFontaine in *Caddisflies* put it this way: "Who carries size 16 imitations of these larvae? Virtually nobody; but these insects can be the predominant organism drifting in the current. The caseless larvae, with no swimming ability, are completely helpless until they regain the bottom."

The pupae also become highly available and important during adult emergence. It's difficult to predict just when hatches will occur in your local streams because of variable conditions and the different species that may be present. In many streams, peak hatch periods occur in the spring and fall, from March through May and September through October. On more than one occasion, I've had masses of *Glossosoma* pupae crawl up my waders hoping to escape the swift water of the riffle I was fishing. Yes, switch to a pupa pattern when this happens.

Not to be outdone by the larvae and pupae, the adults have their own behavior that provides plenty of food for hungry trout. As in several other caddis families, the females dive underwater and swim to the bottom to lay their eggs on submerged rocks in riffles. It seems like a daunting task for such small insects, but one can't argue

with their success; they have survived now for a hundred million years. This also means that stream-loving fish, especially trout, have been eating the egg-laying females of these caddisflies for a very long time.

Glossosoma pupa. DAVE HUGHES

Patterns. The patterns for this group are small, simple, and effective. They are a good example of how important small flies can be and, if you aren't careful, how easy it is to use patterns one or two sizes too large. Using oversize patterns will reduce your success, so pay attention to the actual size of the naturals in the stream you are fishing.

Cream Caddis Beadhead (20–16)

Morrish's Super Pupa (20–16)

Light Tan Flymph (20–16)

LaFontaine Diving Caddis (20–16)

Fishing Tactics. Nymph fishing with the larval patterns is most effective in riffles or the tailouts of riffles where the water deepens. The patterns are small but need to be fished right off the bottom, so adding weight to your leader is required. I prefer the shot and indicator method for this type of nymphing, but if you are fishing pocket water, the high-sticking and Czech methods may be equally or more effective. When imitating pupae and submerged adults, try the Leisenring lift or wet-fly swing. Most of the action will still be in riffles or the area just below them.

American Grannom

Family: Brachycentridae
Major genera: *Brachycentrus, Amiocentrus, Micrasema*

Brachycentrus *larva.* DAVE HUGHES

Micrasema *larva.* JEFF ADAMS

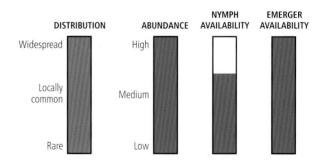

General Information. American Grannom is one of several common names for members of the family Brachycentridae, along with little black caddis, little Grannom, Mother's Day caddis, and little western weedy-water sedge, depending on the species and where you live. Altogether, this family contains three important genera and more than thirty species. The most important species to anglers include *Brachycentrus americanus, B. occidentalis, B. numerosus, Micrasema rusticum,* and *Amiocen-*

trus aspilus. M. rusticum is common in midwestern and eastern streams, and *A. aspilus* is found in western waters. *Brachycentrus* species are the most widespread, with excellent populations occurring all across North America, and are often considered the second or third most important caddis in streams for anglers to imitate, ranking just behind the net-spinning caddis species of *Hydropsyche* and *Cheumatopsyche*.

Brachycentridae are true case builders, constructing well-formed, tubelike cases out of fine plant fibers stripped from underwater vegetation and fine silk threads. Cases come in two distinct shapes; *Brachycentrus* species build four-sided cases that are perfectly square when viewed in cross section, and *Micrasema* and *Amiocentrus* species construct evenly tapered, round cases. Cases of fully grown larvae measure in length from 3/8 inch for *Micrasema* up to 3/4 inch for *Brachycentrus* and *Amiocentrus.* They range in color from olive to dark brown, depending on the material used to construct them. The larvae inside the cases have bright green bodies and dark brown heads and thoraxes.

Pupation occurs inside the mature larva's case. Just before pupation, the larva attaches its case securely to the stream bottom and covers both ends with silk threads. Small perforations in the silk covers allow water and thus oxygen to continue to pass through the case while the pupa develops inside over a three- to six-week period. Hatch periods vary with species. *B. occidentalis* tends to be an early-season emerger, with heavy midday hatches often occurring around Mother's Day, hence its common name Mother's Day caddis. Most other species emerge throughout the summer, with good morning or evening hatches common.

Habitat. Several species of Brachycentridae often occur in the same stream but usually in different habitats. *Brachycentrus* species prefer rocky substrate in moderate to fast riffle areas. *Amiocentrus* and *Micrasema* species, on the other hand, select areas where aquatic vegetation or moss grows in areas of slow to moderate current speeds. As a result, this group of caddisflies occupies a wide variety of streams and different habitats within individual streams, adding to the family's overall abundance and importance. *Brachycentrus* often reaches extremely high abundance in rich, productive tailwater streams like the Bighorn in Montana. Spring creeks with lush beds of aquatic plants can produce equally large populations of *Amiocentrus* or *Micrasema.*

Behavior. Not only is this group widespread and frequently abundant, but its behavior also makes the different stages vulnerable to fish and therefore important to

Brachycentrus *larvae attach their cases to the surfaces of cobble and stones in quick riffles.*

Amiocentrus *and* Micrasema *larvae prefer slower water and areas with aquatic vegetation.*

anglers. The *Brachycentrus* larva feeds by securely attaching its case to the upper surface of a rock on the stream bottom, with the front of the case facing into the current. The larva then extends its legs out of the case and filters food particles from the current. *Micrasema* and *Amiocentrus,* which live in quiet currents, feed by scraping diatoms and algae off the plants where they live. Even though larvae remain inside their cases and seem somewhat protected from trout, they often drift in large numbers. When this happens, trout feed on them, case and all, making cased larva patterns important to anglers. Besides drifting freely in the current, some species of *Brachycentrus* have been noted to navigate from one rock to another downstream by dangling on the end of a long silk thread as if rappelling off a cliff. Though I haven't figured out how to dangle a fly off a rock in a fast riffle, the behavior certainly allows fish an opportunity to feed on the cased larva.

Pupae also give fish plenty of opportunity to feed on them. First they have to swim up to the surface from the stream bottom. Then, though most caddis emerge quickly once at the water's surface, many Brachycentridae struggle with emergence in the surface film for a long time. The result is that pupae and partially emerged adults drift in the film for long distances, giving trout plenty of opportunity to feed on them. After mating, egg-laying females return to the water en masse in the afternoon or evening, leading to wild feeding sprees by trout. Most females lie flat on the surface while laying eggs, but some dive underwater and swim to the bottom to deposit their eggs.

Dense populations of Brachycentrus *larvae can occur where conditions are right.*

Patterns. This may be the most important cased caddis to imitate in the larval stage with the case. Pupae are also extremely important but can be based on typical caddis pupa patterns adjusted to the proper size and color.

Cased Caddis Larva (18–14)

Beadhead Caddis Larva (18–14)

Morrish's HW Caddis Pupa (18–14)

LaFontaine Olive Diving Caddis (18–14)

Fishing Tactics. Drifting larvae should be imitated with cased larva patterns fished right off the bottom. For species of *Brachycentrus* living in swift riffle areas, this means weighted flies, extra split shot, and a strike indicator—in other words, the shot and indicator method. Cover the areas in and around the riffles with the best holding water for trout, trying to visualize where underwater feeding lanes funnel the drifting larvae to waiting fish.

The best action with this group generally occurs when the pupae are swimming up to the surface and adults are struggling to emerge in the surface film. Fishing a dry fly and pupa pattern in tandem can be very effective at this time. Use a dry fly that floats low on the water, and attach a short, twelve- to eighteen-inch dropper to the bend of the hook with a pupa pattern on the end. Fish these with a wet-fly swing through riffles and riffle tailouts where the adults are emerging. Since species of *Micrasema* and *Amiocentrus* live and emerge in slower water with smooth surface currents, lighter gear and careful delicate presentations are necessary to avoid scaring feeding fish.

Cased Caddis

Major families: Limnephilidae, Odontoceridae,
Uenoidae, Lepidostomatidae, Apataniidae,
Leptoceridae
Major genera: Numerous

*Typical Limnephilidae (*Onocosmoecus *sp.) cased caddis
larva.* DAVE HUGHES

Another Limnephilidae larva. THOMAS AMES

Psilotreta *sp. (family Odonticeridae), or dark blue sedge, is
an important cased caddis of eastern streams and rivers.*
THOMAS AMES

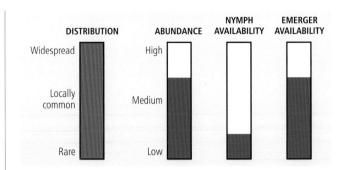

General Information. The real complexity of caddisflies comes into play when dealing with all the different species of cased caddis. Hundreds of species fall into this grouping, yet only a handful become important for anglers to imitate. Even when abundant, many cased caddis are not available as larvae because they do not drift and remain well hidden in the larval cases. Plus, many of the species emerge at night, which practically eliminates the need to imitate pupae or adults. Some of the most important species of cased caddis are listed below, along with their common names, distribution, and general emergence period.

The main challenge with the cased caddis is not knowing when and where a species is important—feeding trout will let you know that—but in trying to put a name to exactly which one happens to be important at any particular time. The problem is really one of identification. If you don't mind ignoring what to call the caddisfly fish are eating and just put on a pattern of the proper type, size, and color to match the naturals, much of the confusion goes away. You still need to carefully observe what stage trout are taking: larva, pupa, submerged adult, or surface adult. Once you solve that puzzle, you should be able to connect with some fish.

Habitat. With the wide variety of species included in this group, the habitat used is also quite diverse. Generally, however, most cased caddis live in water with slow to still current. Such areas are often called depositional zones, because they are places where fine sediment and plant debris such as leaves and small pieces of wood are deposited on the stream bottom. Quiet water near banks and much of the water in pools provide typical depositional zones in most streams. If you look carefully on the bottom in such areas, you will often see dozens of cased caddis larvae crawling slowly along the bottom, with just their heads and legs protruding from their tubular retreats. Because eastern and midwestern streams have more quiet-water habitat than most western trout streams, cased caddis are generally more abundant and important there.

Important Species of Cased Caddis

Family	Species	Common name	Distribution	Emergence period
Apataniidae	*Apatania incerta*	Early smokey wing sedge	East	April–May
Lepidostomatidae	*Lepidostoma* sp.	Little brown sedge	East, Midwest, West	June–Aug.
Leptoceridae	*Nectopsyche albida*	White miller	East, Midwest, West	June–Sept.
Leptoceridae	*Oecetis avara*	Long horn sedge	East, Midwest	July–Sept.
Limnephilidae	*Dicosmoecus* (five species)	Fall caddis or October caddis	West	Sept.–Nov.
Limnephilidae	*Frenesia missa*	Dot wing sedge	East, Midwest	Oct.–Nov.
Limnephilidae	*Pycnopsyche* sp.	Great brown autumn sedge	East, Midwest	Aug.–Oct.
Odontoceridae	*Psilotreta labia*	Dark blue sedge	East	July–Aug.
Uenoidae	*Neophylax fuscous*	Small dot wing sedge	East, Midwest	mid-Sept.–Oct.
Uenoidae	*Neophylax rickeri*	Autumn mottled sedge	West	Sept.–Oct.

Quiet water with fine sediment, aquatic plants, and wood provides excellent conditions for many different types of cased caddis larvae.

Dozens of cased caddis larvae crawl across the stream bottom in a quiet backwater area.

Behavior. That trout feed on case-covered larvae cannot be disputed, but how often they do so and how important they are for anglers to imitate are certainly open for debate. I have rarely found it necessary to imitate cased larvae. When I do catch a fish with a cased larva pattern, I often wonder whether the trout took the fly because it thought it was a cased caddis larva or because the fly also resembled some other insect.

Pupation takes place inside the larva's case. Some larvae burrow into the substrate before pupating, but most species attach their cases to the stream bottom before sealing off the ends. After developing inside the case for four to eight weeks, the pupae wiggle free and swim up to the surface for adult emergence. For many cased caddis, this occurs at night, especially for those species that emerge during warm summer months. Similarly, during the summer, adult activity is often heaviest at night or just before dark and early in the morning. Depending on the species, adults may lay their eggs below the water, on the surface, or even on overhanging vegetation.

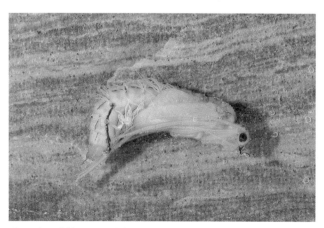

*Cased caddis pupa (*Dicosmoecus *sp.).* DAVE HUGHES

Patterns. Other than some unique patterns to imitate cased larvae, the patterns used to imitate this group are similar to those used for other groups, with the size and color matched to the natural being imitated. Besides pupa patterns, you should have some adult patterns designed to be fished below the surface.

Cased Caddis Larva (12–8)

LaFontaine Emergent Caddis Pupa (12–8)

Copper Bead Caddis Pupa (12–8)

Fishing Tactics. Cased larva patterns need to be fished directly off the bottom. Since most species live in quiet areas with slow current, a weighted fly with no additional weight on your leader is usually sufficient. If you are fishing a large, deep pool, use a sinking line and the count-down method. In water only a few feet deep, the hinged-leader approach can work well. Once pupae start swimming to the surface, use a wet-fly swing or Leisenring lift to match the action of the rising pupae. Pupae of the October caddis, *Dicosmoecus* species, swim along the bottom of the stream until they reach shore, where they crawl up the sides of protruding rocks for adult emergence. Imitate these pupae with a wet-fly swing followed with a strip retrieve along the bank once the fly has swung close to shore. A wet-fly swing also imitates adults that dive underwater to lay their eggs, then drift slowly back up to the surface.

TRUE FLIES: Order Diptera

This order was named Diptera, meaning "two wings," because the adults have only two wings instead of the four present in other insect orders. Diptera is a huge order rivaling beetles in terms of overall species diversity, with more than 120,000 described species worldwide and nearly 18,000 known in North America. It includes many everyday insects, such as houseflies, horseflies, and mosquitoes. Unlike the other orders described in this chapter, in which all species are aquatic, the majority of true fly species are terrestrial. Still, there are more than 3,500 aquatic species of Diptera in North America alone—more than all the species of mayflies, stoneflies, and caddisflies combined. Perhaps fortunately for fly fishers, many aquatic Diptera species have adapted to environments unsuitable for trout and many other gamefish and therefore need not concern the angler. Even so, though Diptera are often considered of lesser importance by the fly fisher, hundreds of species thrive in trout streams and form an important part of the fish's diet, and there are many occasions when Diptera are the dominant food and must be imitated correctly for the angler to have any chance at catching fish.

Several factors increase the importance of aquatic Diptera to fly fishers. First, true flies, like caddisflies, undergo complete metamorphosis and pass through four stages of development: egg, larva, pupa, and adult. But unlike caddisflies, a complete life cycle for many aquatic Diptera takes only a few months to complete, and a species may have two, three, or even four generations a year. Thus important hatches often occur several times a year, increasing the frequency at which fly fishers need to imitate different stages. Second, with the large diversity of aquatic Diptera, some species live in every conceivable type of habitat. Areas less desirable to the mayflies, stoneflies, and caddisflies, such as slow-flowing reaches with sandy or silty bottoms, are often heavily populated by Diptera species. Therefore, in streams or sections of streams with few of the big three present, Diptera are often abundant and readily available to fish.

The behavior of many aquatic Diptera also increases their availability to feeding trout. Larvae usually develop on the stream bottom, either attached to the surfaces of stones or hidden below deposits of silt or debris, and most are poor swimmers. It would seem, then, that they would rarely be available to fish, but in fact, many aquatic Diptera larvae drift in large numbers and day in and day out are often the dominant species drifting in the current. Pupation occurs either underwater along the stream bottom or out of the water in damp areas along the shore. Pupae that develop underwater generally leave the stream bottom when mature and drift slowly up to the surface for the adults to emerge. Other species emerge underwater, and the adults rise up to the surface. Like the larvae, pupae swim poorly and are readily available to trout when rising to the surface. Adults are also available either underwater or on the water's surface, depending on where the species emerges.

Recognizing Diptera species is relatively easy at the order level. Most larvae have no legs. When legs are present, they are not true jointed legs on the thorax, but short, single segmented structures called prolegs, generally attached to the underside of the abdominal segments. On many larvae, the head is highly modified, being reduced in size and sometimes withdrawn inside the first thoracic segment. These larvae appear to be headless and look like simple segmented tubes. Gills may be absent or present, and when present occur in various shapes and locations. Pupae are best recognized by the segmented abdomen and fat thorax with stubby wing pads. Short fleshy or filamentous gills often protrude near the pupa's head. Adults have only two wings. The second pair has morphed into short, clublike structures called halteres, which spin in flight like miniature gyroscopes and keep the insect on an even keel. The size and color of larvae, pupae, and adults vary tremendously. The biggest headache for fly fishers is the small size of most aquatic Diptera, usually size 20 or smaller, though some species are well over an inch long. As for color, anything goes, including red, green, yellow, orange, black, gray, silver, and brown.

Out of the thousands of aquatic Diptera species, the most important to the fly fisher fall into four families: Chironomidae, the midges; Tipulidae, the craneflies; Simuliidae, the blackflies; and Athericidae, the snipe flies. Learn to recognize when these groups are abundant and being eaten by trout, and then choose an appropriate pattern to match them. Given their tiny size and the selective ways trout often feed on them, this can be easier said than done. In many ways, aquatic Diptera create the ultimate fly-fishing challenge.

Midges

Family: Chironomidae
Major genera: Numerous

Chironomid larvae look like simple segmented tubes.
DAVE HUGHES

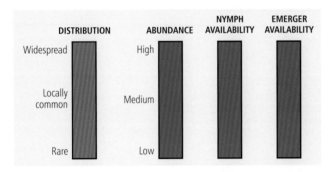

General Information. Widespread, abundant, and available, the family Chironomidae, the midges, can't be ignored, even though I often would like to. The problem with this group is threefold. First, because most species are very small, it can be difficult to tell when trout are eating them and at what stage. Second, trout often feed on midges selectively even when more obvious insects are present and abundant. And third, trout often take midges in quiet water where they can carefully inspect the naturals and your imitations. Thus success requires light lines and tippets, careful presentation, and well-matched patterns. In a nutshell, the tiny midge can create a big challenge for the fly fisher.

Identifying midges beyond family is next to impossible for anyone but a trained taxonomist specializing in midges, so I will not discuss important genera or species for this group. The best guess is that there are more than a hundred genera and two thousand species in North America alone, with new species routinely being discovered. For the fly fisher, simply recognizing the family is adequate for selecting a pattern.

Midge larvae have slender, curved bodies with a pair of prolegs just behind the head and at the tip of the abdomen. The head is small but distinct. Pupae are also simple in form. The body is evenly tapered, with distinct but short wing pads at the thorax and a pair of small, paddlelike plates at the end of the abdomen. Most species have a clump of short, white filamentous gills on top of the head. Adults are slender with relatively long legs, and males have noticeably bushy antennae. In many ways, adult midges look like mosquitoes, but fortunately they lack biting mouthparts and are harmless.

Midges come in a wide range of sizes and colors, and the color of the larvae, pupae, and adults of the same species may differ. Therefore, if you suspect fish are selectively taking one of the stages of a midge species, it is important to collect the natural to determine what size and color you need to match. This is the first, and often the biggest, problem to solve. Though I am not a fan of

Chironomid pupa hanging in the surface film before adult emergence. DAVE HUGHES

Adult chironomid adult emerging in the film. DAVE HUGHES

stomach pumps and do not advocate their use, as too many fish are harmed by anglers using them, if you manage to catch a fish, pumping its stomach will confirm whether trout are taking midges and, if so, what stage, size, and color. As an alternative to using a stomach pump, hold a fine-meshed insect-collecting net in the current for a few minutes where you have seen fish feeding. If midges are prevalent in the drift, you should be able to collect a few that you can then match with an appropriate pattern. Note: If you're over forty-five years old, put on your reading glasses when looking into the net, or you'll never see these little guys.

Habitat. Midge species have adapted to nearly every type of aquatic habitat. Pick up a rock from a fast riffle, and if you look closely, you will almost always find little silken tubes that often look like slender lines of silt across the surface of the stone. Midge larvae live there. Pull up some aquatic plants, and you will find a variety of midge larvae living both on and inside the plant tissue. Grab a handful of silt and mud from the bottom of a quiet pool, drop it in a tray of water, and in a few seconds you will see midge larvae wiggling out of the muck. One thing you can be sure of, whether you are fishing spring creeks, large rivers, or little streams, is that midges are present. Pupation occurs in the same habitat used by a particular species of larvae. Pupae typically remain well hidden on the stream bottom until mature, which takes only a week or less. Adults emerge in the surface film, then fly to nearby vegetation. Swarms of adult midges can often be seen over streamside grass or shrubs as they prepare to lay their eggs on the water's surface or by crawling underwater.

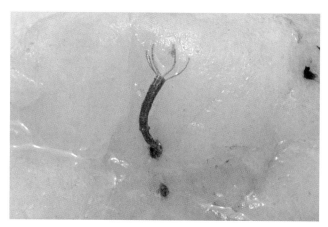

Some midge larvae live in small, tubelike cases attached to the surface of rocks or debris.

Behavior. The most important behavior of midges to the fly fisher is their propensity to drift. Nearly every insect drift study I've seen has found midge larvae or pupae the most abundant or close to the most abundant organism drifting. This doesn't mean they are always important to imitate, since other insects also drift in large numbers and may attract more attention from the fish. It does mean that midges of some type are almost always there for fish to eat.

Though larvae readily drift and can be worth imitating, I find pupae even more available and important to imitate when they rise up to the surface during a midge hatch. They are poor swimmers and move slowly up to the surface. Once there, they may hang in the film for a minute or longer before the adult starts wiggling free of the pupal exoskeleton. Throughout this period, pupae are extremely vulnerable to trout or any other fish wanting an easy meal. Given that the number of pupae drifting during a hatch can be quite high, trout often become selective to them, necessitating an imitation matching their size and color.

One hundred to two hundred midge species are often collected from just a single section of stream that's carefully studied, and with so many different species present in any individual stream, midge hatches occur every week of the year. This is well known to anglers who venture forth in the winter and routinely find midge pupae and adults riding the currents and trout sipping them with dainty little rises in or just under the surface. If you fly-fish, sooner or later you will be faced with imitating midges.

Patterns. The number of midge patterns developed by fly tiers is second only to the number of midge species living in streams and lakes. The most important features of any midge pattern are its shape, size, and color. Midges are always slender, so your fly pattern should be sparse and slender also. Many patterns try to capture the translucent quality of emerging pupae with different types of materials. The pattern is only part of the answer, however; a good presentation is just as important for success.

Miracle Midge (22–14)

Brassie (22–14)

Olive Beadhead Midge Pupa (22–14)

Chan's Frostbite (22–14)

Maroon Beadhead Midge Pupa (22–14)

Miracle Midge Pupa (22–14)

Fishing Tactics. Midge patterns are small, so this is one nymphing situation where light lines of 4-, 3-, or even 2-weight are appropriate, along with fine leaders. Since midges live in every kind of stream habitat, you will find yourself fishing their patterns in a range of water types. The best tactics to use depend on the water you are fishing and how deep trout are feeding. When they are taking pupae in or just under the film, an up-and-across dead drift presentation generally works. A lot of good midge activity occurs in gentle or slow-flowing waters where you can spot feeding fish. The Sawyer method works well in this situation. When you can't see the fish, using a small indicator or dry fly can help you track your fly and detect takes. The hinged-leader technique is a good choice when fishing deeper in slow-flowing waters. In faster water, the shot and indicator approach can be used effectively. In all cases, strikes will be gentle and difficult to detect.

Craneflies

Family: Tipulidae

Major genera: *Hexatoma, Limonia, Dicranota, Antocha*

Tipulid larva. DAVE HUGHES

Antocha larva. JEFF ADAMS

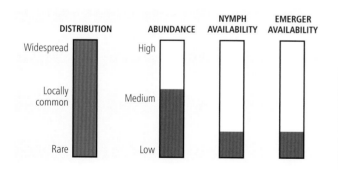

General Information. Craneflies are probably most familiar to people as the large, long-legged bugs that flit around porch lights on warm summer nights and are often referred to as mosquito hawks. This variety happens to be terrestrial, its larvae living under the soil in gardens or lawns, where they can become a pest if you enjoy green grass. The larvae of almost six hundred cranefly species also happen to live in streams across North America. The family is widespread, and it would be rare to find a stream without a few species of craneflies. Their abundance and availability vary, however, and their importance to fly fishers is sporadic, especially in comparison with the midges.

Not all craneflies are the size of the large mosquito hawks. Depending on the species, fully grown larvae may range from less than 1/4 to almost 2 inches long. Those most important to anglers tend to be 1/4 to 1/2 inch long as both larvae and adults. For some reason, those that warrant imitation most often also happen to be the smallest species. Colors vary little among species, with light tan to dark brown the usual range for all stages.

Larvae and pupae are rather basic in shape. A simple tubelike body characterizes larvae. Some species have prolegs along the underside of the abdomen, but many other species don't. Most characteristic of cranefly larvae is the apparent lack of a head. Though present, it is tucked deep inside the first thoracic segment and completely hidden from view. At the same time, the last abdominal segment of some species has the interesting habit of swelling into a round, bulblike shape. With no head visible, most people think the swollen rear end of the body is the front end the first time they see a cranefly larva. Pupae look like simple segmented tubes with a swollen thorax where the legs and wing pads are tucked tightly together. Most species require one year to complete their life cycle.

Habitat. The majority of cranefly species live in marginal trout habitat, preferring muddy areas along banks or stagnant backwaters. This reduces their availability to trout and minimizes their importance to anglers. When flows increase during spring runoff or heavy rains, however, high water can wash these big, juicy larvae from their secure hiding spots and offer fish an easy meal. Some species, primarily those of the genus *Antocha,* have adapted to living on rocky substrate in swift currents of cool streams, which increases their availability to trout and importance to anglers. Except for a few species, pupae develop in shallow backwaters or moist soil on the banks and are not available to fish. Adults, which hang out on streamside vegetation until ready to lay their eggs, may be the most available of the three stages.

Behavior. Larvae cannot swim, so they move slowly along the bottom. Depending on the species, their food may range from decaying plant matter to small insects. Since many larvae live in quiet, often shallow backwater areas, they do not frequently drift in the current where trout will see them. Except for species of the genus *Antocha,* which live in swift water, the best time for trout to find cranefly larvae is when they get washed out of their quiet areas during high-water events. Likewise, pupae are rarely available to fish, given their development in moist, shallow areas along the bank. The exception is again species of *Antocha,* which are midstream emergers. But it's not the pupae that are available. The adults emerge from the stream bottom while the pupal cases remain attached to the substrate. It is therefore the adults that trout see, with their long gangly legs moving in the current, drifting underwater until they break through the water's surface. At other times as well, the most available stage of craneflies is the adults. Warm summer days and evenings often find them in large numbers hovering along shoreline vegetation or around the exposed tops of midchannel rocks. The females of some species crawl underwater along the sides of the submerged rocks to lay their eggs, then get washed into the current, where trout can easily pick them off. Others get blown into the water by the wind and drift across the surface, where trout sometimes take them with noisy splashy rises.

Patterns. Only a couple simple nymph patterns are needed to cover this group. Large sizes are best during high water; small patterns will match the swift-water species of *Antocha.*

Top: *Tipulid Larva (12–8);* bottom: *Beadhead Pupa (16–14)*

Fishing Tactics. Craneflies are not an important group to imitate very often. I find the best periods are during high water. A medium to large cranefly nymph pattern fished deep along the edges of the stream, where trout get relief from the main force of the current during high water, can result in some nice fish. The shot and indicator approach works well in most of these situations. You might also find periods when emerging *Antocha* adults are present in good numbers or drifting underwater after laying their eggs. A small pupa pattern or tan soft-hackle will often match submerged adults. Fish these flies with a Leisenring lift or wet-fly swing.

Blackflies

Family: Simuliidae
Major genera: *Simulium, Prosimulium*

Blackfly larvae. JEFF ADAMS

Blackfly larva and pupa. JEFF ADAMS

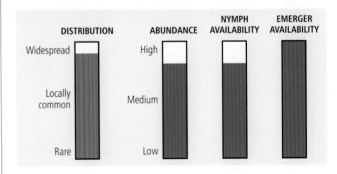

General Information. Besides blackflies, insects of the family Simuliidae are also called buffalo gnats or reed smuts and are the perpetrators of the frustrating smutting rise. I suspect many anglers know blackflies better for the pain received from them than for the trout caught on their imitations. When the adults are out in full force and looking for blood, no one is immune to their relentless attacks. For some reason, most blackfly species in northwestern and most western streams do not have the same bloodthirsty attitude as their midwestern and eastern cousins. Why, I don't know, but it became exceedingly clear to me during a June trip through the mountains of New Hampshire and Maine some years ago. I pulled into a campground to fish a small stream. Even though it was over 90 degrees, everyone had on a long-sleeved shirt, long pants, and a hat with a head net. Strange, I thought, as I got out of the car in my shorts and T-shirt and waded into the pleasantly cool water. I released a small brown trout and was still wondering why everyone was so overdressed when a cloud of small flies appeared and descended on me. They immediately covered every exposed area of my body and quickly ran under my T-shirt and up my shorts. The little buggers even crawled into my nose and ears. Blood trickled down the side of my face as I reached my car, jumped inside, and sped off to somewhere far away from that little bit of hell pretending to be a trout stream.

Blackflies are distributed worldwide. In North America, more than 150 species have been described. The larval and pupal stages are aquatic and generally prefer swiftly flowing water. All stages are small, with most species ranging from $1/4$ to $1/8$ inch long. It is hard to understand how such small adults can inflict such painful bites. Larvae are shaped like tiny bowling pins. The bottom of the abdomen has a circle of small hooks that grip a patch of silk threads they place on the substrate. When firmly attached, they can hold on in the full force of the current. During the summer or in warm-water streams, larvae mature in only a couple of weeks. Pupae look like little tan slippers topped with a crown of slender gill filaments. Pupae complete their development in only four or five days. Adults leave the pupal cases underwater and float to the water's surface encased in small bubbles of air. Mating may occur on land or in the air. Females that bite do so because they require a blood meal for their eggs to mature. In tropical climates, the whole life cycle may take only a few weeks. In temperate regions, species may complete one to six generations a year.

The importance of this group to anglers comes into play when larvae drift in the current and when adults rise to the surface during their emergence, creating the well-known smutting rise, a reference to one of the common names for this group, reed smuts. The classic example of a smutting rise is trout sipping something unseen just under the surface film of a clear spring creek, though this activity can occur in many types of streams. Drifting larvae can be quite prolific at times and thus become the target of feeding trout. Blackflies are second only to blue-winged olives in availability to trout. As for abundance, blackflies tend to be very spotty in their distribution. Some areas of a stream can be covered with larvae and

pupae while other, similar-looking spots have none. It takes careful observation and experience to know when trout are taking these little pests.

Habitat. Blackflies live in all types and sizes of streams and rivers, and many species prefer the same conditions trout look for: cold water with moderate to fast currents. The larvae are able to grip the substrate in the fastest water and can be found clinging to rocks, wood, and the leaves and stems of aquatic plants. Most larvae seek areas in the main force of the current; where conditions are right, thousands are often clumped together in just a square foot or two of stream bottom. The pupae attach to the bottom in the same fast-water areas where larvae live.

Blackfly larvae and pupae attached to rock

Behavior. Most blackfly larvae have a unique mode of feeding that requires them to sit in the full force of the current. On top of the head is a pair of rather unusual structures called labral fans that are held out into the current. In this position, the fine hairs strain small drifting food particles from the water. With their butts attached firmly to the substrate and their heads sticking up into the current, the larvae have managed to find a niche used by few other insects. Even though the larvae have a secure grip on the substrate, they often drift. At times, this is done by dangling in the current on a silk thread as if rappelling from one rock to another.

The pupae, in their small cocoons, stick tightly to the bottom and rarely enter stream drift. The adults burst out of the pupal cocoons underwater and float up to the surface encased in small bubbles of air. Their rise to the surface offers plenty of chances for trout to intercept them. The females of some species crawl underwater down the sides of wood debris or rocks to lay their eggs, after which they drift once more underwater. Other species lay their eggs on the water's surface.

Patterns. For some reason, European and English fly fishers seem to have developed more patterns for blackflies than anglers in North America, even though blackflies are no less common here. Perhaps the greater number of other aquatic insect species in most North American trout streams has overshadowed these tiny insects. The best way to determine whether blackflies are being eaten is to hold a fine-meshed net in the current for several minutes. With any luck, you will be able to see exactly what is drifting downstream. If it is a blackfly, choose a larva or subsurface adult pattern as appropriate.

Tungsten Midge (24–18)

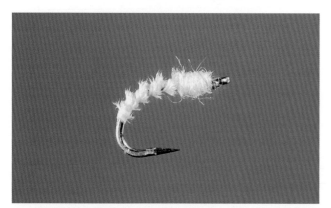

Cream Midge (24–18)

Tailwater Tiny Rust (24–18)

Fishing Tactics. Try a dead drift presentation at the depth where fish are feeding. In clear water where you can spot the fish, the Sawyer method works well. In other waters, the hinged-leader method can be a good choice. Or attach fifteen to twenty-four inches of tippet off a dry fly as a dropper, and let the dry be your indicator. With the very small flies required to imitate blackflies, light lines and fine tippets are in order.

Snipe Flies

Family: Athericidae
Major genus: *Atherix*

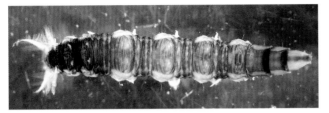

Snipe fly larva. JEFF ADAMS

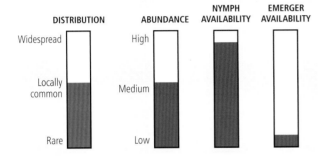

General Information. The family Athericidae, the snipe flies, has received little mention in the fly-fishing literature. That may be an oversight, as this family of Diptera can be locally abundant and the larvae are readily available to trout when present. The family has only two genera and four species, but they occur in streams and rivers all across North America. I find them in most streams I collect in, though they are generally low in abundance. A trip to Rock Creek in western Montana, however, proved that snipe flies can be one of the most abundant and important insects in the stream. It was early July, and I decided to take my own advice and collect a few insect samples from the stream before selecting a pattern and beginning to fish. There were a number of nice riffles with pocket water and deeper runs. It seemed just the right environment for mayflies like blue-winged olives and pale morning duns, plus stoneflies and lots of net-spinning caddis larvae. My collecting turned up a surprise, however. I did find mayflies and a number of different stoneflies, but virtually no caddisflies. Instead, snipe fly larvae wiggled and flipped everywhere in the net. Since no hatches were happening, it was obvious what to imitate. Like most anglers, I had no snipe fly larva imitations in my vest, but fortunately a size 12 Green Rock Worm Nymph looks very similar. That nymph proved to be just the ticket, hooking fat west-slope cutthroat consistently for the three days I was able to fish.

Snipe fly larvae range from about 1/2 to just under 3/4 inch long when full grown. They are rather slender and,

like all Diptera, have no true legs. Instead, they have eight pairs of short, stubby appendages called prolegs along the underside of the abdomen. Off the rear end, a pair of moderately long lateral filaments stick out like short tails. The front end tapers to a point, and the head, highly reduced in size and hidden within the first thoracic segment, is virtually invisible. Most specimens I have collected are dark olive to rather bright green.

Neither pupae nor adults are important to imitate, as they occur where trout cannot get at them. Pupation occurs on land, and adults lay their eggs on vegetation overhanging the water, successfully avoiding most trout in the process.

Habitat. The three species of the genus *Atherix* are the most important to the fly fisher, as they occur in riffles of cold-water streams and rivers—in other words, the same places as trout. To pupate, the larvae leave the water and select a damp spot along the bank, where they dig an inch or two under the soil.

Riffles and runs with cobble bottom provide the right conditions for snipe fly larvae.

Behavior. Snipe fly larvae are predators. This means they need to actively move along the stream bottom in search of prey. As a result, they commonly end up in stream drift and become available to feeding trout. Another characteristic of the larvae causes them to stand out rather dramatically: When placed in a tray of water, they twist with rapid, convulsive twitches. This movement makes them hard to miss in a sample tray of stream insects, and it may make them hard for trout to miss as well. Larvae can't swim and simply drift close to the stream bottom until they can regain a foothold on a rock or other debris. Mature larvae must migrate to shore in order to crawl out for pupation, and this also increases their exposure to fish. Adults are predaceous on other small insects but do not bite people.

Snipe Fly Nymph (14–10)

Patterns. Simple green rock worm patterns tied in shades of brown, olive, and green will nicely match most snipe fly larvae. The larval stage is the only one you need to imitate.

Fishing Tactics. Since snipe fly larvae live in riffles and drift along the stream bottom, any nymphing tactic used for fishing near the bottom in fast water will work. The shot and indicator, high-sticking, and Czech methods can all be effective, depending on the specific type of water being fished. Your fly or leader needs to have enough weight to drift your nymph right off the stream bottom.

The right fly and the right technique will produce fishy results like this fat westslope cutthroat trout.

SCUDS AND SOW BUGS: *Aquatic Crustaceans*

Crustaceans dominate the world of arthropods in salt water. In fresh water, they take a backseat to aquatic insects in terms of arthropod diversity, with about eleven hundred species of freshwater crustaceans known in North America. Crustaceans can be quickly distinguished from insects by their two pairs of antennae and jointed appendages on the thoracic and abdominal segments. The head and thorax frequently appear joined and together are referred to as the cephalothorax. Though insects change dramatically in shape and function between life cycle stages, immature and adult crustaceans look and behave the same; they vary only in size and reproductive ability. Thus crustaceans have no hatches and remain aquatic throughout their entire life cycle.

Many freshwater crustaceans, such as cladocerans and copepods, are planktonic and, though eaten by fish, are much too small to be used as models for fly patterns. Others, however, are large, abundant, and available enough to provide important food for fish, and their imitations can be the key to taking trout. Two groups of freshwater crustaceans, sow bugs (order Isopoda) and scuds (order Amphipoda), are especially of interest to the fly fisher.

Don't forget to take time to smell the flowers; just be careful where you put your nose. Though bee-like in appearance, this common occupant of streamside flowers is harmless. It is a member of the Diptera family Syrphidae, appropriately called flower flies.

Sow Bugs: Order Isopoda
Family: Asellidae
Major genus: *Asellus*

Isopod, or sow bug. DAVE HUGHES

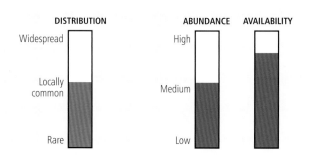

General Information. Most species of sow bugs, also called pill bugs, are terrestrial or marine. More than a thousand species are found in North America, but only about eighty live in fresh water. Of these, ten are widely distributed across the country. Many others have adapted to local conditions and may occur in a single spring or stream. The abundance of sow bugs also varies locally and can range from none to thousands per square meter. Some studies have shown higher numbers of sow bugs in waters with higher concentrations of calcium and dissolved solids.

Sow bugs are dorsal-ventrally compressed, which means flattened from top to bottom as if they have been stepped on. Two pairs of antennae, one long and one short, extend forward from the front of the head, and each of the seven thoracic segments sprouts a pair of well-developed legs. Body colors range from dark brown to tan, olive, reddish, or yellowish. The size of adults may range from $1/4$ to $3/4$ inch long. Except for size, there is virtually no difference between newly hatched young and adults. During their one-year life cycle, individuals may molt fifteen or more times, and females may lay one to two broods of eggs before dying.

Habitat. Sow bugs occur in many types of streams, but the best populations occur in areas with slow to moderate currents. Most prefer clean, unpolluted water and often reach their greatest abundance in spring creeks that have rich growths of aquatic vegetation. Sow bugs like to hide under rocks, wood debris, or vegetation and generally prefer water less than three feet deep.

Thick beds of aquatic vegetation often harbor large numbers of sow bugs.

Behavior. Sow bugs are poor swimmers and move by crawling across the substrate with their long legs. They are primarily scavengers, feeding on decaying animals and plants. Given their preference for slow water and their poor swimming ability, they do not drift in large numbers. When abundant, however, trout seem to look for them, and fishing their imitations can be very effective. Since both immatures and adults are aquatic and live in the same habitat, they remain present throughout the year, with abundance varying seasonally following periods of mating and the emergence of new young.

Patterns. Effective nymph patterns for sow bugs can be quite simple. Since the size and color of sow bugs differ among streams, it is helpful to collect a few naturals where you are fishing so you can select a matching pattern. Most species live in shallow, slow water, so these nymph patterns do not need to be heavily weighted.

Sow Bug Nymph (16–10)

Fishing Tactics. Relatively shallow water, less than three feet deep, with slow to moderate current speeds typify the kinds of locales where you will fish sow bug imitations. Nymphs should be presented near the bottom with little or no action. These conditions favor the hinged-leader or shot and indicator approach. The Czech method, with its short line and sensitive detection of strikes, can also be effective where you can approach fish closely without spooking them.

Scuds: Order Amphipoda

Major families: Gammaridae, Talitridae
Major genera: *Gammarus, Hyalella*

Amphipod, or scud. DAVE HUGHES

*Amphipod (*Gammarus *sp.).* JEFF ADAMS

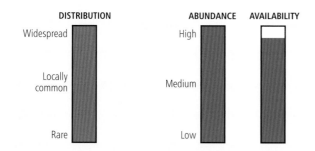

General Information. Members of the order Amphipoda provide an important source of food for trout and other fish in many streams, rivers, lakes, and ponds. Besides the common name scud, these creatures are also called freshwater shrimp or side swimmers. Like most crustaceans, the majority of species are marine. Across North America, there are about ninety species of freshwater amphipods. Species of the genera *Gammarus* and *Hyalella* produce most of the fishable populations in streams and lakes in North America.

Scuds and sow bugs often occur together in the same waters, but scuds are almost always more abundant. They also inhabit a wider variety of waters than sow bugs and thus become important to imitate more often. Scuds and sow bugs are similar in size and often overlap in color, but several obvious differences make them easy to distinguish. Scuds are laterally compressed, flattened from side to side as if their right and left sides were pressed together, unlike the top-to-bottom compression of sow bugs. They also can swim quite well. Like sow bugs, scuds have a pair of legs on each of the thoracic segments, but they also have a pair of appendages on each of the first three abdominal segments that they use for swimming. As for food, scuds are also scavengers and eat all types of dead animal and plant matter.

Young and adults occur in the same areas and look identical except for size. After eight molts, individuals are sexually mature, and adults may continue to molt fifteen to twenty more times. The complete life cycle typically lasts one year. Many species produce a single brood of eggs as adults, but *Hyalella* females may mate and lay as many as fifteen broods of eggs, with about twenty eggs in each brood. Amphipods can be extremely abundant, with populations of more than ten thousand individuals per square meter occurring in ideal habitats. In many streams, scuds are the go-to food to imitate when other patterns fail. Sizes and colors may vary widely from stream to stream. Most scuds range from $1/4$ to $3/4$ inch long and may be shades of gray, brown, olive, or orange.

Habitat. Amphipods have adapted to a wide range of moving and stillwater habitats, with the best populations found in clean, cold, unpolluted waters. Good numbers occur in fast riffle sections with a rocky substrate, as well as slower-water reaches with a silt bottom. Some of the best populations occur in spring creeks where aquatic

Slow to moderate currents with aquatic vegetations and wood debris provide excellent conditions for amphipods.

vegetation is abundant. River reaches below dams that provide uniform temperatures, consistent flows, and thick beds of aquatic plants also produce large scud populations. Most species prefer shallow water, but one species has been collected as deep as three hundred meters in Lake Superior.

Behavior. In contrast to the slow-moving sow bugs, scuds swim well and seem to be constantly on the go. As a result, scuds enter the drift more often than sow bugs and are generally more available for trout to eat. Scuds dislike bright light, so they often hide in thick vegetation or under rocks and debris during the day, then come out at night to forage for food across the bottom. Therefore, your best fishing opportunities with scud patterns are often first thing in the morning or late in the evening, when shadows cover the water, or on dark, overcast days.

Scuds mate anytime between February and October, depending on water temperature. Paired males and females often swim in tandem for several days before mating. After mating, the fertilized eggs are held by the female in a special pouch called a marsupium for one to three weeks. Newly hatched young remain in the marsupium for another one to eight days before being released.

Patterns. Scud patterns are standard flies in most anglers' arsenals for good reason: They are simple to tie and consistently catch fish. Given that young and adult scuds occupy the same water and behave the same way, scud imitations can be effective all year long. As with sow bugs, the size and color of individual scuds from different streams may vary widely, so collect a few naturals before choosing a pattern.

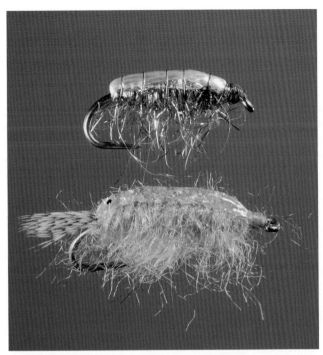

Top: *Copper Scud (14–10);* bottom: *Amber Epoxy Scud (14–10)*

Fishing Tactics. Amphipods occur in a wider variety of habitats than sow bugs, but their patterns should still be presented near the bottom with little or no action. Depending on the water type, you might find the shot and indicator, hinged-leader, high-sticking, or Czech method most effective. Using a scud pattern as the point fly when fishing two or three nymphs together can be an excellent tactic when scuds and several other aquatic insects are abundant.

The following table summarizes the importance and pattern selection for the twenty-eight major groups of insects discussed in chapter 6. Use this table as a general guide and as a quick reference for finding the detailed information discussed in the book.

Insect Importance and Pattern Summary

Insect group	Common name	Importance in western waters	Importance in eastern waters	Patterns	Pattern size range	Details on pages
Ephemeroptera	*Mayfly*					
Baetis	Blue-winged olive	*****	*****	Pheasant Tail Krystal Flash Baetis Skip Nymph Krystal Flash Baetis Emerger Smurf Emerger	20–16	99–101
Siphlonurus	Gray drake; black drake	*	***	Feather Duster Gray Drake Mercer's Poxy Back	12–8	101–2
Ameletus	Brown dun	***	*	Near Enough Theo's CDC Brown Devil	12–10	103–4
Isonychia	Great leadwing	**	***	Gray Drake Isonychia Nymph	10–8	104–5
Ephemerella	Pale morning dun	*****	*****	Flashback Hare's Ear Skip Nymph PMD Emerger Partridge and Orange CDC PMD Emerger	18–14	106–8
Drunella	Flav	****	*****	Olive Beadhead Hare's Ear Flashback Beadhead Hare's Ear Pheasant Tail	14–10	109–10
Drunella	Western green drake	***	*	Beadhead 20-incher Possie Bugger Ida May CDC Green Drake Emerger	12–8	111–12
Paraleptophlebia	Mahogany dun	****	****	Copper John Trina's Bubbleback Emerger CDC Pheasant Tail Beadhead Emerger Brook's Sproat Emerger Lawson's Floating Nymph	18–14	113–14
Tricorythodes	Trico	***	***	Trico Nymph Trico Spinner Wet	24–18	115–16
Heptageniidae	Quill Gordon; March brown; light cahill	****	*****	March Brown A. P. Olive Mercer's Poxy Back March Brown Flymph	16–12	117–19
Ephemeridae	Hex; brown drake; eastern green drake	**	****	Extended Body Burrower Nymph Hexagenia Nymph	8–6	120–21

(continued on page 164)

Insect Importance and Pattern Summary (continued)

Insect group	Common name	Importance in western waters	Importance in eastern waters	Patterns	Pattern size range	Details on pages
Plecoptera	***Stonefly***					
Nemouridae	Little brown stone	**	**	Little Brown Stone Nymph Matthew's Amber Stone Nymph Pheasant Tail Soft-Hackle	16–12	123–24
Chloroperlidae	Little green stone	***	***	Light Tan Beadhead Hare's Ear Olive Flymph	16–12	124–25
Perlodidae	Little yellow stone	****	****	Mercer's Gold Dust Beadhead Red Squirrel Nymph Smurf Stone Partridge and Yellow Soft-Hackle	16–10	126–27
Perlidae	Golden stone	*****	****	Mercer's Brown Stone John's Beadhead Golden Stone Beadhead Brook's Stone Smurf Stone	12–6	128–29
Pteronarcidae	Giant stone	****	**	Brook's Stone Black Stone Smurf Stone	12–4	130–31
Trichoptera	***Caddisfly***					
Rhyacophila	Green rock worm	*****	****	Beadhead Krystal Flash Caddis Beadhead Green Rock Worm Green Rock Worm Morrish's Supper Pupa LaFontaine Deep Sparkle Pupa Translucent Diving Caddis	14–10	133–35
Hydropsyche, Cheumatopsyche	Net-spinning caddis	*****	*****	Net-Spinning Caddis Barr's Gold-Bead Net-Spinning Caddis Zug Bug Tan CDC Flymph LaFontaine Emergent Sparkle Pupa CDC Beadhead Pheasant Tail Emerger	16–12	135–38
Philopotamidae, Psychomyiidae	Lesser net-spinning caddis	***	****	Beadhead Caddis Larva Cream CDC Flymph Mercer's Z-wing Caddis Silvey's Prime Pupa Tan	20–14	139–40
Glossosoma	Saddle-case caddis	*****	****	Cream Caddis Beadhead Morrish's Super Pupa Light Tan Flymph LaFontaine Diving Caddis	20–16	141–43

Insect Importance and Pattern Summary (continued)

Insect group	Common name	Importance in western waters	Importance in eastern waters	Patterns	Pattern size range	Details on pages
Trichoptera	*Caddisfly*					
Brachycentridae	American Grannom	*****	****	Cased Caddis Larva Beadhead Caddis Larva Morrish's HW Caddis Pupa LaFontaine Olive Diving Caddis	18–14	143–45
Limnephilidae, Odonticeridae, Uenoidae	Cased caddis	***	*****	Cased Caddis Larva Cased Caddis Pupa LaFontaine Emergent Caddis Pupa Copper Bead Caddis Pupa	12–8	146–48
Diptera	*True fly*					
Chironomidae	Midge	*****	*****	Miracle Midge Brassie Chan's Frostbite Miracle Midge Pupa Olive Beadhead Midge Pupa Maroon Beadhead Midge Pupa	22–14	150–52
Tipulidae	Cranefly	**	**	Tipulid Larva Beadhead Pupa	16–8	153–54
Simuliidae	Blackfly	**	***	Cream Midge Tungsten Midge Tailwater Tiny Rust	24–18	154–56
Athericidae	Snipe fly	***	**	Snipe Fly Nymph	14–10	157–58
Crustaceans						
Asellidae	Sow bug	**	***	Sow Bug Nymph	16–10	159–60
Gammaridae	Scud	****	****	Copper Scud Amber Epoxy Scud	14–10	161–62

* = Rarely important; ** = Occasionally important; *** = Commonly important;
**** = Frequently important; ***** = Almost always important

Everyday Nymph Patterns

Clearly, a wide variety of patterns are used to imitate the different types of insects common in streams and rivers. You might be wondering if there is a core set of nymph patterns that effectively imitates the most important naturals. Such a set would greatly simplify the number of nymph patterns one would need to carry. In fact, most experienced anglers do have a core set of dry-fly, wet-fly, and nymph patterns that have proven effective for them over the years. While the specific patterns will vary among anglers and from one region of the country to another, most will be flies that can represent multiple types of naturals. A Gold-Ribbed Hare's Ear nymph tied in different sizes, shapes, and colors, for example, can imitate numerous types of mayflies, several types of stoneflies, a few different caddis, and even roughly match a scud or sow bug. Many new patterns are really just slight variations of proven general patterns.

Since there is no single short-list of nymph patterns anglers have agreed to, I have provided a list of my own favorite everyday nymph patterns. From my experience, these twelve patterns, tied in the range of sizes and colors indicated, are effective in streams and rivers throughout North America and beyond. Selecting which pattern, size, and color to use should still be based on an understanding of what naturals are most abundant where and when you are fishing. These aren't the only nymph patterns I carry, but they will give you a good idea of how to put together a fly box for successful nymphing.

Still too many patterns for you? Well, if a wizard stranded me on the banks of a trout stream with a choice of only four nymph patterns, I would want a size 18 Pheasant Tail, size 16 brown Beadhead Gold-Ribbed Hare's Ear, size 12 Krystal Flash Green Rock Worm, and size 10 dark brown Smurf Stone.

1. Beadhead Gold-Ribbed Hare's Ear: Tan, brown, and olive in sizes 16–10.

2. Pheasant Tail: Natural color in sizes 20–12.

3. Zug Bug: Natural color in sizes 16–10.

4. Beadhead Red Squirrel: Natural color in sizes 16–10.

5. *Beadhead Krystal Flash Caddis: Dark olive to bright green in sizes 14–10.*

6. *Smurf Stone: Black, brown, and gold in sizes 12–4.*

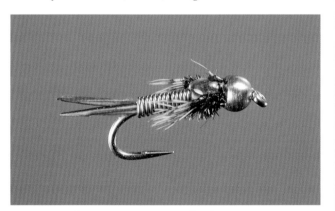

7. *Copper John: Copper, green, and red in sizes 20–12.*

8. *Cased Caddis: Tan, dark brown, and dark olive in sizes 12–8.*

9. *Scud: Tan, olive, and orange in sizes 16–10.*

10. *Flymphs: Yellow, orange, green, olive, and tan in sizes 18–12.*

11. *CDC Beadhead Emerger: Dark brown, tan, olive, and yellow in sizes 18–10.*

12. *LaFontaine's Deep Sparkle Pupa: Brown, green, and yellow in sizes 16–10.*

CONCLUSION

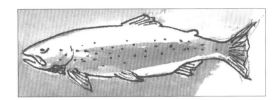

Iwoke early and walked down to the river. The slanting rays of morning light cast long shadows across the still, glassy surface. I'm always amazed how lifeless a river can look when no insects or fish disturb the water. As terrestrial beings, we rely on the water's surface to inform us about activity below, and yet we know that it hides from us more than it tells. Roderick Haig-Brown, in his book *A River Never Sleeps,* got it right: No matter how asleep a river may look, below the surface sleep never comes. Thousands upon thousands of nymphs and larvae let go of the stream bottom and float downstream every day as part of the early-morning behavioral drift cycle. Trout move into their favorite feeding stations and quietly begin the day with a meal of the dominant nymphs that drift into view then quickly disappear—nature's own version of fast food.

The experienced angler understands how the surface can be deceptive and enters the water knowing that below the surface trout are feeding. Earlier sampling of the insects in the stream has revealed what nymphs are most likely on the trout's breakfast menu. Using a nymph pattern to match the naturals, the angler casts so the fly sinks into the hidden feeding lanes along the stream bottom. As the fly drifts downstream unseen, the angler visualizes a trout moving close to the fly and is ready to set the hook at the slightest change in movement of leader or indicator. With the angler's knowledge of the insects, fish, and nymphing tactics put into play, it is only a matter of time before a fighting trout breaks the surface stillness.

Whether you're new to fly fishing or a longtime angler trying to better understand nymph fishing, all the information about insects, fish, and tactics may seem like a lot to learn. That's because there is a lot to nymph fishing. The fact that you have to understand what occurs below the surface, where you can't see what's happening, makes nymph fishing more challenging—and often more frustrating—than just about any other method of fly fishing. Learning basic nymph-fishing skills, however, will greatly improve your fishing success. And there is no reason you can't master them. Just don't expect to do it in one day, one week, or even one season. Be patient and practice the methods described in this and other books on the subject.

Darrel Martin, fly-fishing author and superb tier and angler, told me many years ago how, in the current world of specialization, fly fishing is one of the few activities that still successfully combines art and science. Nymph fishing is a perfect example of this. It involves science in the study and understanding of insects, fish, and fishing methods, as well as art in the form of fly patterns, the act of casting and presenting a fly, and the beauty of rivers and the trout they hold. Every fly fisher experiences this combination of art and science every day on the water. First, we use thought and analysis to select a fly and decide where and how to fish. Then, standing in the river, with all of the life it provides above and below the water, we experience the inescapable beauty and wonder of nature along with the art of fly fishing. Above all, I hope this book has helped you better understand the science and further appreciate the art of nymph fishing.

Happy nymphing!

BIBLIOGRAPHY

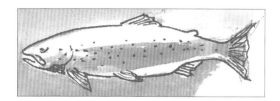

Ames, Thomas, Jr. *Hatch Guide for New England Streams.* Portland, OR: Frank Amato Publications, 2000.

Arbona, Fred L. *Mayflies, the Angler, and the Trout.* Tulsa, OK: Winchester Press, 1980.

Brooks, Charles E. *Nymph Fishing for Larger Trout.* New York: Crown Publishers, 1976.

Caucci, Al, and Bob Nastasi. *Hatches: A Complete Guide to Fishing the Hatches of North American Trout Streams.* Woodside, NY: Comparahatch, 1975.

Edmunds, George F., Jr., Steven L. Jensen, and Lewis Berner. *The Mayflies of North and Central America.* Minneapolis: University of Minnesota Press, 1976.

Hafele, Rick, and Scott Roederer. *An Angler's Guide to Aquatic Insects and Their Imitations.* 2nd ed. Boulder, CO: Johnson Books, 1995.

Hafele, Rick, and Dave Hughes. *The Complete Book of Western Hatches.* Portland, OR: Frank Amato Publications, 1981.

———. *Western Mayfly Hatches.* Portland, OR: Frank Amato Publications, 2004.

Harris, J. R. *An Angler's Entomology.* New York: A. S. Barnes and Co., 1952.

Hughes, Dave. *Trout Flies: The Tier's Reference.* Mechanicsburg, PA: Stackpole Books, 1999.

———. *Handbook of Hatches.* Mechanicsburg, PA: Stackpole Books, 2005.

Hynes, H. B. N. *The Ecology of Running Waters.* Toronto: University of Toronto Press, 1970.

Kaufman, Randall. *American Nymph Fly Tying Manual.* Portland, OR: Frank Amato Publications, 1975.

Kite, Oliver. *Nymph Fishing in Practice.* Shrewsbury, UK: Swan Hill Press, 2000.

Knopp, Malcolm, and Robert Cormier. *Mayflies: An Angler's Study of Trout Water Ephemeroptera.* Helena, MT: Greycliff Publishing Co., 1997.

LaFontaine, Gary. *Caddisflies.* New York: Lyons & Burford, 1981.

Leisenring, James E., and Vernon S. Hidy. *The Art of Tying the Wet Fly & Fishing the Flymph.* New York: Crown Publishers, 1971.

Leiser, Eric, and Robert H. Boyle. *Stoneflies for the Angler: How to Know Them, Tie Them, and Fish Them.* New York: Alfred A. Knopf, 1982.

Martin, Darrel. *Micropatterns: Tying and Fishing the Small Fly.* New York: Lyons & Burford, 1994.

McCafferty, Patrick W. *Aquatic Entomology.* Boston: Science Books International, 1981.

Merritt, Richard, and Kenneth Cummins. *An Introduction to the Aquatic Insects of North America.* 3rd ed. Debuque, IA: Kendall/Hunt Publishing Co., 1996.

Migel, Michael J., and Leonard M. Wright, Jr., eds. *The Masters on the Nymph.* Guilford, CT: The Lyons Press, 2002.

Richards, Carl, and Bob Braendle. *Caddis Super Hatches: Hatch Guide for the United States.* Portland, OR: Frank Amato Publications, 1997.

Rosborough, E. H. *Tying and Fishing the Fuzzy Nymphs.* Harrisburg, PA: Stackpole Books, 1978.

Schollmeyer, Jim. *Hatch Guide for Western Streams.* Portland, OR: Frank Amato Publications, 1997.

Schollmeyer, Jim, and Ted Leeson. *Trout Flies of the West: Best Contemporary Patterns from the Rockies, West.* Portland, OR: Frank Amato Publications, 1998.

———. *Trout Flies of the East: Best Contemporary Patterns from East of the Rockies.* Portland, OR: Frank Amato Publications, 1999.

———. *Tying Emergers.* Portland, OR: Frank Amato Publications, 2004.

Schwiebert, Ernest. *Nymphs: A Complete Guide to Naturals and Their Imitations.* New York: Winchester Press, 1973.

Skues, G. E. M. *The Way of a Trout with a Fly.* London: A & C Black, 1921.

Sternberg, Dick, David Tieszen, and John van Vliet. *Fishing Nymphs, Wet Flies & Streamers.* Minnetonka, MN: Creative Publishing International, 1996.

Stewart, Kenneth W., and Bill P. Stark. *Nymphs of North American Stonefly Genera (Plecoptera).* 2nd ed. Columbus, OH: The Caddis Press, 2002.

Swisher, Doug, and Carol Richards. *Selective Trout.* New York: Crown Publishers, 1971.

Ward, J. V. *Aquatic Insect Ecology: 1. Biology and Habitat.* New York: John Wiley & Sons, 1992.

Whitlock, Dave. *Dave Whitlock's Guide to Aquatic Trout Foods.* New York: Nick Lyons Books, 1982.

Wiggins, Glenn B. *Caddisflies: The Underwater Architects.* Toronto: University of Toronto Press, 2004.

———. *Larvae of the North American Caddisfly Genera (Trichoptera).* 2nd ed. Toronto: University of Toronto Press, 1996,

INDEX

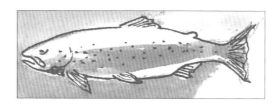